'Building the Pyramid is shortlisted for tł Year.'

Chartered Management Institute in a C000122449
School and the British Library

'An excellent teaching tool.'
Charles Handy, author and business philosopher

'This is not just another 'how to' book on delivering a strategic plan. John Stein draws on the power of storytelling to influence and inspire using one of the greatest organisational development challenges known to man. He shares his tried and tested winning (formula)® to take us on a highly valuable learning journey, maximising the leadership potential in us all.'
Professor Laurie Wood, former Executive Director, Enterprise and Development, University of Salford

'Our verdict – a FIVE STAR RATING. In contrast to the many heavyweight business books, the style of the book is easy to get into and would work well as a teaching aid for managers in any organisation.'
Talk Business Magazine

'In the past decade our business has grown tenfold. John and his original book deserve much credit. The core messages in the updated *Building the Pyramid* are the same but subtly improved. It's a first class read, easy to follow with simple messages – a clear vision, engage with your people, culture is everything. Business leaders will benefit from reading and using the lessons it shares.'
David Pollock, Chief Executive Officer at Chess Telecom

'Stein has certainly done his historical homework, but it's in the small nuggets of general management wisdom where he's most enlightening.'
CIPD People Management Magazine

'John Stein's wealth of experience has been packaged into this 'leadership route map' and I think anyone reading this easily accessible volume will gain a number of great insights – or a whole template for their own journey.'
Lloyd East, Regional Chief Executive Officer at RSA Middle East

'John's use of an iconic universally known structure and its construction to explore leadership, change and success has real impact. All the tips and examples are relevant today and extremely useful in helping to understand the complex nature of the subject. A very easy read and a book I thoroughly recommend.'

Peter Coley, Head of Learning at St Mungo's Broadway

'*Building the Pyramid* is an informative and insightful book highlighting the leadership behaviours and activities required to achieve success on the growth journey. It should be shared with everyone connected with an organisation when there is a need to launch a new journey or refresh and refocus colleagues on an existing one.'

Adele Ventre-Downey, HR Consultant and former Head of HR at Alternative Futures Group

'*Building the Pyramid* is a concise, compelling and different read for any business leader. Most of all, it captures the challenges we all encounter on our journeys whilst we strive to build our own pyramid. The book is also much more than a leadership tool. Rarely do you find a leadership framework that is relevant outside senior management, yet *Building the Pyramid* is relevant for the whole team to be engaged in the journey, without exception.'

Ian Blackhurst, Chief Executive of entu UK plc and co-owner of Sale Sharks Rugby Club

'Recommended reading.' **HR Grapevine Magazine**

'If you are intent on creating something special, if you are committed to a growth journey or a period of change within your business then I would urge you to pick up a copy. The framework behind the book is tried and tested – I know because I have been part of the success it has driven.'

Joe Haworth, Commercial Director at Job Worth Doing

'Stein has been using the story of how a pharaoh builds his own pyramid as the basis for a successful leadership training course. It's an interesting approach and he covers a lot of ground in the book's 128 pages.'

Scottish Business Insider Magazine

'I found *Building the Pyramid* an inspirational and compelling read. There is a phrase in the book 'simple is powerful' and John Stein has managed to achieve this in abundance.'

Patricia Walsh, Global Chief HR Officer at Squire Patton Boggs

'*Building the Pyramid* is an essential part of any business leader's tool box. It articulates clearly how to adapt to change, which is a constant in today's business world. You can easily take elements of the book, or adapt the whole roadmap contained in the story to improve your leadership skills enabling effective engagement across your team.'

Les Torrance, Senior Director at Sykes Global Services

'John Stein's unique vision and insight has been captured in an easy-to-follow format. A must read for any entrepreneur seeking clarity in the chaotic business world of today.'

Will Rees, Entrepreneur and Director at Direct Online Services

'John Stein's winning formula approach to navigating the 'business growth journey' is enlightening, insightful and pragmatic. *Building the Pyramid* explains how to communicate your plans, engage, develop and motivate everyone connected with your business. It also demonstrates how to maintain people's enthusiasm and appetite towards helping you achieve your goals. John's insight into the modern business is nothing short of genius and his approach is proven many times over.'

Chris Morrisey, Managing Director at Lily Comms

'April Book of the Month.' **HRDirector Magazine**

'*Building the Pyramid* is a truly memorable book using a simple story to great effect to highlight a practical business growth model. It gives structure to thinking and planning for the difficult things including getting buy-in, creating vision and ultimately achieving success.'

Nicola Bramwell, Managing Director at Qaigen Ltd

'There is no denying the value of the message and guidance this book provides. It's very entertaining, it's simple and it's common sense.'

Ray Davis, Category Judge, Chartered Management Institute

'Unusual but quirky! the book brings into play tactical and operational approaches to dealing with moving the journey along and this is supported by a range of materials late in the book from case studies to fifty important points to remember to deliver success on the journey.'
HR Network Scotland Magazine

'I found the book a real goldmine of fresh thinking. It provided a waffle-free insight and prompted me to think differently (and I hope better) about how my colleagues and I can get things done effectively via people. Highly recommended and a real 'find''
Fred Best, HR Business Partner at National Oilwell Varco

'This book really is a must read for anyone interested in business – it offers not only tips on running a company but explains why particular changes and ideas are important. It is cleverly written, inspirational and includes many messages which stay with you long after you finish reading the book.'
Charlene Feeney-Seale, Senior Associate Consultant at PwC

'*Building the Pyramid* is ideal for forward-thinking leaders, particularly those with an entrepreneurial focus. HR professionals will also benefit from the insight it offers about the role of the leader on the journey and the use of John Stein's winning formula framework in helping to inspire, manage and deliver change. The first step to gaining wisdom is realising that we may not have it. *Building the Pyramid* will ask lots of rich questions about your own journey and help you to identify many of the answers.'
Carl Fitzsimons, Group HR Director at MW Brands

'John Stein has found a unique way of simplifying, into six key stages, the multifarious components involved in engaging an organisation to achieve a common goal – namely Growth! We have found this framework essential in guiding our people towards our £100m sales target – which we achieved in 2014! If you are a leader, serious about Growth, *Building the Pyramid* is a 'must read' but be prepared to be challenged…'
Gary Dewhurst, Founder and Chief Executive Officer at gap Personnel

Building the Pyramid

-

The winning (formula)® approach to
delivering success on your
organisation's growth journey

Best wishes on the chess business growth journey !

John Stein

John Stein

-

TWF Publications

First Edition

This edition published in Great Britain by
TWF Publications
Dallam Court
Dallam Lane
Warrington
WA2 7LT
www.the-winning-formula.com

A CIP catalogue record for this book is available from the British Library.

ISBN 9780954713416

Book cover by Chay Hawes
Typeset by Craig Martin

"It soon became obvious that we
were but on the threshold of the discovery"

Howard Carter

Contents

Introduction

Steering an organisation on its unique growth journey is one of the biggest personal challenges facing all leaders. Although the end goal, the destination may stay the same, the conditions experienced on the journey will be different within six months, and different again within a year.

Why? Because internal and external issues and events will constantly change the commercial landscape in which the organisation operates.

Navigating the landscape has become the new core requirement of the 21st century leader. To support this need, meet the challenges ahead and deliver success, a more flexible, adaptable leadership approach is needed to keep everyone connected with the organisation on track – a framework that adapts to changing conditions on the journey.

The winning (formula)® is a powerful performance framework with a proven track record of equipping leaders and managers with the knowledge and skills required to successfully grow, develop and transform the fortunes of their organisation.

Building the Pyramid describes the workings of the framework and how it can be applied to help leaders and their teams succeed on their journey.

The Journey Context

Journeys are a part of all of us. We spend most of our lives on a journey to somewhere, whether a change of location, a career path, even a new relationship.

We start out dreaming of the future, full of hope and ambition. We set off into the unknown with fear and excitement. We experience despair and frustration but also overcome the most difficult hurdles. We celebrate key milestones and dine out on reaching seemingly impossible goals.

Is that life or business? The answer is either. The growth journey is no different to any other life journey, and is just as rewarding.

However, very few leaders view the workplace experience in the context of a journey. The day-to-day pressures of managing the organisation can get in the way of thinking of work as anything other than an intense process of actions, activities and decisions. More's the pity.

All leaders dream of building a successful, growing and sustainable organisation. Likewise, their teams dream of being part of the same workplace experience.

Pursuing that dream should be seen as an adventure for everyone connected with the organisation. The journey to achieving sustainable growth should be lived and enjoyed by all, and this includes suppliers, partners and other stakeholders.

As this book will show, purpose and a sense of belonging are important to everyone in every organisation. They make the difference between people merely going through the motions or giving their all. With everybody feeling a connection to the growth journey, morale improves, productivity increases, efficiency improves, retention rates remain high. People are more engaged.

In the commercial world the positive impact on sales revenue, profit and cash – the most important requirements of any growing organisation and the aspects that dominate leaders thoughts on a daily basis – are immense.

The Need for a Framework

The challenges to running any organisation and steering it on a growth journey are of course, manifold. You know that remaining competitive is important to your long-term success. Managing the expected growing pains, improving operational efficiency, implementing change, improving the customer experience, engaging your people and developing a high-performing culture will form part of your overall strategy.

On top of that, you are faced with three main leadership challenges that will dramatically affect your organisation's performance.

These are:

1. Developing and leading a vision for the organisation to which everyone will commit

2. Aligning strategy to operational goals and objectives

3. Executing the strategy and delivering the plans for growth

Address each of these areas successfully and your growth journey will surpass your expectations.

But this is all easier said than done. You and your fellow leaders may have a clear vision for the organisation in your mind. But does everyone else in the company share that vision, in order for it to become a reality?

Your strategy might sit nicely with your operational goals on paper, but what happens if a major competitor steals market share, throwing your operational goals to the wind? Will your leadership be as effective in the face of the pitfalls that might lie ahead?

The reality is there will be many events to throw you off-course. Economic conditions will play their part, markets will change, key people will leave when you least expect it and internal conflicts may come to a head.

The most important role for the leader is to keep everyone on track, and guide them through these constantly shifting sands. To do that, you need a framework.

A framework allows people to stay focused on the task ahead rather than worrying about the changing view out of the window. When people are focused on the task, they are united in achieving it and confident in doing so.

Without a framework, the temptation will be to tackle each obstacle as it comes. That sticking plaster approach may be right for the time and satisfy an immediate need, but it does not offer a long-term solution that will contribute to the development of a sustainable growing organisation. That is the essence of a framework.

This book highlights how it can be achieved.

The winning (formula)®

The winning (formula)®, as demonstrated in *Building the Pyramid*, is a simple, unique and powerful performance framework that focuses on the six most important areas of strategic and operational focus required by leaders and others on the growth journey.

1. The six areas are as follows:

2. The attraction and recruitment of talent

3. The alignment of strategy to operational performance

4. The engagement of others via the development of leadership capability

5. The creation of a strong workplace-performance climate

6. The powerful use of knowledge, expertise and talent via learning

7. The demonstration of behaviours important to maximising the organisation's potential

Leadership focus on these areas will guarantee success.

The six-stage award-winning approach enables leaders to:

- Understand the commercial landscape and the challenges facing them on the journey

- Produce a route map to help them navigate others to their destination

- Enlist support and commitment from others to the plans for growth

- Execute the strategy and deliver the goals and objectives set for the organisation

- Maximise the potential and talent of each individual in the organisation

- Build an agile, successful and sustainable organisation

The approach has enabled our clients to achieve spectacular growth results – in excess of £500 million of additional revenue and resulting profits.

The framework is research-based, tried, tested and proven to work for leaders in small, medium-size and large organisations. And it is no sticking plaster. It is no management fad or initiative. It continues to be used by many of our clients nearly a decade after they were first introduced to it.

Why the success? In 1995, we decided to embark on our own unique journey and try to understand what really worked in the world of business. We spent years researching the world of leadership, strategy, engagement, performance, motivation and growth.

And we also researched people and their attitude to work. We needed to understand individuals and what made them tick – even more so now, with the 'Facebook generation' of socially aware, inter-connected individuals entering the workplace and into leadership and management positions.

It wasn't easy to get right. We tried and failed, tried again and succeeded, and then tried and failed again. And we kept on trying until the winning (formula)® became the powerful approach that it is today.

Victor Hugo once said 'simple is powerful' and this applies to our framework. We have stripped away what we believe are the factors which get in the way of delivering growth and have produced an approach which has delivered spectacular results for our clients.

The framework is flexible in terms of its use by leaders in any organisation. It can be used in a linear step-by-step basis when an organisation wishes to embark on a new and exciting growth journey; the appointment of a new leader, a change in strategic direction, a merger, acquisition or the need for a fresh start, for example.

Alternatively, it can also be used tactically by leaders to re-energise and re-focus the people in their organisation at key moments on their journey on any of the six areas highlighted in the formula.

The winning (formula)® approach to delivering performance and growth will transform your organisation and the people working in it. The framework will enable you to create and lead a truly inspirational organisation.

Format of the book

Building the Pyramid demonstrates the winning (formula)® framework in action, through the use of a simple story set in ancient Egypt. It is an original interpretation of the challenges facing leaders and how success can be achieved. The storyline format of the book is also supported by leadership learning points, visual interpretations of the journey landscape, personal exercises and checklists, as well as information from clients on their use of our framework over the past few years.

Lessons learned on the Pharaoh's journey include how to:

• Attract, recruit and retain talent

• Lead the 'change' required to deliver success

• Harness the power of vision and values

• Increase levels of engagement across the organisation

• Build a positive workplace culture

• Align strategy to operational performance

• Inspire others to maximise their potential

More importantly, *Building the Pyramid* demonstrates how to successfully navigate colleagues on the journey towards the creation of a more agile, successful and sustainable organisation.

One of the most energising journeys any person can experience is the growth journey.

Best wishes on your journey, wherever it may take you.

John Stein
Founder of the winning (formula)®

The Pyramid as a Metaphor for Growth

Great leaders know the power of a good story. People are moved by emotion, not spreadsheets or orders. A good story that captures the imagination will do far more to motivate a workforce than providing them with reams of dry business data. As an extremely powerful, visual way of conveying important messages, storytelling is being adopted by leaders the world over.

The idea here of a story based on a pyramid and its construction came from the striking similarities between this symbol of endurance, power and strength and the requirements of organisations in today's world.

The pyramid is probably the best example of ancient precision engineering known today. As a design icon, its shape is perceived as elegant and timeless. And indeed, with eighty such structures still in existence, they have truly stood the test of time – an impressive feat and pertinent to *Building the Pyramid*.

Built primarily as the final resting-place for a deceased Pharaoh, a pyramid also helped transfer him or her on the journey to the next world. Each Pharaoh was ambitious and demanding, requiring unique creative twists that would differentiate his pyramid from those built before.

Building the pyramid was a massive undertaking, involving a cast of thousands. The pyramids, contrary to public belief, were not built by slaves but by highly skilled craftsmen including masons, carpenters, plasterers and painters. The Egyptian subjects were happy to participate, believing that the pyramid would immortalise their King and would ultimately bring them good fortune.

But how were they built and what lessons can leaders take from the pyramid builders? A lot more than you might first think.

The Parallels

In many ways, there is a direct correlation between the 'Pyramid Building Journey' of the Pharaoh and the 'Growth Journey' of the modern-day leader.

To begin with, the Pharaoh and the leader shared a common single-minded determination to create something totally unique.

The Pharaoh's desire was to build a monument that could not only transfer him to the New World, but would be a dynamic place where his people could relax, worship, and proudly say 'we built that'.

In the case of forward-thinking leaders today, the desire is to build a solid and successful organisation, which can be differentiated from competitors and others. Many aim to create an outstanding business, where 'above average' growth becomes the norm. Like the pyramid, the organisation enables people to say 'we built that'.

Secondly, the pyramid building 'journey' towards completion involved six key phases. Our winning (formula)® approach to delivering performance on the growth 'journey' also involves six key stages.

Both journeys involve the initial development of a vision by a single person. Leadership plays a critical role in the development, support to and realisation of any vision, whether you are a Pharaoh or a Chief Executive.

Although the story is based in ancient Egypt, the highs and lows experienced in organisatons today could easily echo the events, experiences and outcomes involved in the building of the pyramid over four-thousand years ago.

Finally, it could take twenty years to build the pyramid, meaning that few Egyptian people had previous experience, and the workforce would constantly change during its construction. People were therefore asked to take a leap of faith and trust the leader (the Pharaoh), his officials and the journey. The workforce of an organisation today with new, ambitious and exciting plans for growth are similarly asked to trust the leaders, many of whom have little experience and knowledge in the unique dynamic of growing an organastion.

Linking Past and Present

The issues raised in this tale of ancient Egypt will resonate strongly with today's leaders. That is no coincidence. It is because they mirror the results of countless employee surveys that we have conducted on behalf of our clients over many years.

We fully understand the workplace issues facing leaders, employees, partners and others today, and in *Building the Pyramid*, my aim was to bring these issues to life, demonstrating how leaders can navigate their own path on the growth journey, no matter when or where they start.

The high officials from ancient Egypt faced the same people challenges of modern-day leaders. Little has changed between the building of an Egyptian pyramid and that of an organisational pyramid. Behaviour delivers performance, therefore leadership focus on the right behaviours will always deliver growth, success and sustainability.

But you have to begin the process by embarking on a new journey, with a renewed sense of purpose supported by a real sense of adventure.

Modern-day leaders can learn a great deal from the Pharaohs. Next time you see a pyramid, reflect on the reasons for embarking on the journey, the vision required to create it, and the role of the leaders in navigating their landscape to make sure it was completed.

Enjoy the story.

Building the Pyramid

Advice to a Pharaoh

The Pharaoh had been ill for several months and knew she did not have long before she would make her next and final journey, from life to death. The sun-god Osiris was, she hoped, ready to receive her. She had ruled the Kingdom of Egypt for over twenty-five years, and in that period had maintained Egypt's position as the wealthiest country in the world.

The people loved their Queen and she had served them well. From the start of her reign, she was an ambitious and fairly demanding Pharaoh, one with a clear idea of what needed to change. Now at the end of her reign, she was equally clear on the planning required for her death.

The most important part of this meticulous planning involved the building of her pyramid, which had taken some sixteen years to complete. The Royal Architect had designed a truly impressive monument. An enthusiastic workforce, happy to help the Pharaoh plan for her journey to the stars, had completed the pyramid ahead of schedule.

The final part of the Pharaoh's preparation involved a meeting with her son, the young Prince, who would follow in his mother's footsteps. On her death, he would be crowned Pharaoh in turn. The Prince, called Smendes, was a fine young man but whether he was ready to rule was, at least to some, a matter of concern. The Queen hoped to address this by imparting some of her long-developed wisdom.

The Pharaoh called Smendes over.

"You have learned a great deal in my reign and I hope you are ready to receive the crown and the throne," she began. "When I have passed to the next life, there are three things you must do. If you carry them out, you will have a successful reign and a peaceful and harmonious life as the King."

"The first thing you will need to do is to look after your people and they, in turn, will look after the kingdom. You may soon be the ruler of Egypt, but without the support of your people you will never achieve great things."

While he felt this was fairly obvious, the young Prince nodded in agreement.

"Secondly, begin the process of building your own pyramid as soon as you are King, because the construction could take up most of your reign. The task will be fraught with challenges, frustrations and many difficulties; you must persist though, to ensure your own passage to the next world."

"Finally," she continued, "In building the pyramid, you will need a strong and capable team of advisers, scholars and officials. The best advice I can give you is to spend time with a man you will not yet have met. He is known by some as the Sage or the True Scholar. He is wise in many things and is the man, above all others, who will help you. He holds the secrets to building the pyramid. He has the formula; talk to him son," the Pharaoh said.

The young Prince was confused as to who this man was, but he could see the Pharaoh tiring, and decided he would tackle his mother the following day.

He kissed her goodnight and whispered "I will see you tomorrow."

His mother looked at him: "Remember my advice," she replied.

In the middle of the night the Pharaoh died. The young Prince was woken to be given the news, and handed a papyrus copy of his mother's final words, written by her physician.

The inscription read: 'Great is a great one whose great ones are great.'

It would take Smendes many years to appreciate the significance of those words.

When it came to the late Pharaoh's funeral, the meticulous planning she had carried out with the Prince and the court officials ensured that the ceremony was conducted exactly as she would have wished.

The Pharaoh's body began the journey from her palace, along the Nile on the Royal Barge. Thousands lined the banks, paying their last respects to a beloved Queen. Her coffin was taken into the Queen's Chamber within the pyramid and lowered into the Sarcophagus, surrounded by prized possessions, gifts to the gods and materials designed to support the success of her journey.

The young Prince's new journey began with his return to the palace for a banquet celebrating the life of the deceased Pharaoh. After the banquet, he received each guest and personal condolences were offered.

At the end of the procession of guests was one man who was particularly eager to meet the Pharaoh to be. This was the person of whom his mother had spoken.

When his turn came, the scholar bowed deeply before the Prince.

"Your mother was a great woman; she will be sadly missed," he said in a deep, slightly accented voice.

"True," the young Prince replied. "See the number of people who have turned up today to wish her well on her journey."

"Why do you think so many people wish to honour her?" asked the Sage.

The Prince was surprised by the question, but replied, "because she was the Pharaoh, and because she was loved."

"Indeed, sir," replied the Scholar with a slight smile, knowing that there was more to it than this.

"Please tell me how I should address you?" asked the Prince, eager to make progress. "My mother said you are called the True Scholar or the Sage, but you must have a name."

"Your mother always addressed me by my family name, Prem, which was my preference as I am not an enthusiastic adopter of titles."

"Then," said the Prince, "I think we'll use that. My mother told me before she died, that I should come and talk to you. I believe that you sometimes offered her advice. Will you give the same service to me?"

"When you are ready sir; you have a great deal to do in the next few months. I will be happy to speak to you when the time is right." Again he bowed to the younger man.

"Then I will contact you," said Smendes.

"As you wish sir," although Prem knew this would prove to be untrue. He shook the Pharaoh's hand and left.

Ten days later, the coronation took place and Smendes was crowned Pharaoh, supreme ruler of his people and the most important and powerful man in all of Egypt.

He began his reign remembering his mother's advice to look after the people, build the pyramid right away and consult with the Sage.

Regarding the people he felt that, as long as he continued with his mother's policies, this would be sufficient. His officials assured him that the people were happy and content.

He would, therefore, concentrate his efforts on the building of his pyramid and would begin that journey later on in the year. He was determined that his would be the perfect pyramid, a magnificent structure unlike anything previously created. Contrary to his mother's advice though, he did not intend to use Prem – after all, why should he? As a prince, he had been trained for the role of Pharaoh and had spent many hours in the company of his mother and her advisers, listening to them as they planned her pyramid. He knew more about pyramid building than any scholar did.

He spent the remainder of the year assembling his team of managers and advisers, arguably the most important part of his planning process. He had learned that the strength of this team would reflect the strength of his workforce and, ultimately, the quality and standard of his pyramid.

His team would involve a mixture of youth and experience. Some of his mother's people would be invited to take up positions on the project, alongside new blood.

He started with the appointment of his architect, an expert in pyramid design. Other appointments followed swiftly and a team of specialists and scholars covering disciplines such as tool making, food, clothing, safety, storage and security supported his senior advisers.

In keeping with his mother's advice to 'look after the people', he appointed an expert to attend to the needs of the workforce.

One of the older advisers asked if a plan would be produced to help focus everyone's minds on their great task.

The Pharaoh replied that he had confidence in their abilities and that there was no need to spend time on an unnecessary exercise. A Pharaoh had never produced a plan before and he wasn't about to start now.

The following morning he announced to the people of Egypt that they were about to embark on a new journey, to build the Pharaoh's pyramid.

Construction Commences

The building of the pyramid got off to a great start. The people were delighted that they were embarking on the new Pharaoh's journey and were keen to demonstrate their support for their King.

The architect had, true to his word, designed the perfect pyramid and, with the help of astronomers, had found the ideal location.

The building of the pyramid was to involve six phases and the architect knew that the first, laying the foundations, was the most important. This would take at least two years to complete and the people set about the task with energy and enthusiasm.

The construction operation was organised and well managed. Within two years, and according to the schedule agreed with the Pharaoh, the first phase was completed. The foundations were laid and now the hard work was about to begin. This would involve more stone, more transport and considerably more people – an extra seventeen thousand in total.

The Pharaoh called for the people of Egypt to support the next stage of the pyramid construction. Conscription had existed within the kingdom for many years and it was every Egyptian's duty to enlist. The Pharaoh therefore anticipated a positive response, but to his horror and surprise found that only two thousand people supported his call to action. This would take the total workforce to five thousand, far short of the figure needed to complete the work on time.

The royal advisers were as surprised as the Pharaoh with the low response but, as they were too involved in their day-to-day jobs, were unable to understand or explain the reasons why.

After three intense weeks spent in further recruitment the workforce was up to strength, although there was still no real explanation for the initial reluctance to join up.

The Pharaoh could now relax, confident that the pyramid construction would remain on schedule. The work picked up pace. Everyone played his or her part and the pyramid began to take shape.

One day, the Pharaoh decided to visit the quarry and then the pyramid site to check the progress. He was delighted with what he saw and decided to extend the visit and greet the people personally. Everyone seemed happy and, when asked, informed the Pharaoh that all was well.

He returned to the palace a contented man. However, the harsh truth was that, although the people may have had the appearance of being busy, they were merely going through the motions.

They were supporting the Pharaoh's journey with a reasonable standard of work but the passion and pride was missing. They knew they had to support the journey but they had serious reservations about the new Pharaoh.

Many found him abrupt, cold and aloof. They also felt isolated from him. Since the coronation, he had left the palace only twice to meet them. As a result, rumours began to surface regarding his intentions for the kingdom and plans for the future.

At a personal level, food wasn't quite as plentiful as it had been and, although there wasn't a major crisis, it was commonplace to go several weeks without certain foodstuffs. Wives spent less time with their husbands; children saw less of their fathers. Families were being affected by the long hours the men spent on the construction of the pyramid.

They vented their frustrations on their superiors who, in turn, notified the Pharaoh's advisers. Nobody, however, was brave or confident enough to inform the Pharaoh of the people's concerns.

Ironically, the Pharaoh's last visit to the site had increased the work rate for a few days, but then it slid back at an alarming rate. Four years into the journey, the building of the pyramid fell behind schedule.

Smendes summoned an urgent meeting of his managers and advisers. He reminded them in no uncertain terms that, as ruler of Egypt, he was able to command his people to move mountains.

"So why are you unable to get your people to carve, move and place a few pieces of stone?" he asked them.

This was a deeply insulting remark. It understated the complexity and size of the project and, at the same time, undervalued the advisers and other officials.

He asked them each to list the various problems linked to their area of responsibility and, when they did so, he responded by offering them solutions to bring the construction back on schedule. The mood of the meeting was both tense and quiet. The team was frightened to speak out and offer any input to the process. This only made the Pharaoh angrier.

"Tell the people they have a duty to their Pharaoh!" he shouted. To their horror, the Pharaoh went on to personally ridicule each of the team members, questioning their ability and blaming them for the situation he was in.

One of the scribes was told to complete a detailed summary of the Pharaoh's required actions, including who was responsible and the timescales involved. The Pharaoh concluded by informing them that failure would not be tolerated, and that his concerns should be communicated to their workers.

The officials left the meeting angry, frustrated and bewildered. Many feared for their jobs, and some for their lives. By the end of the day, twenty thousand people were aware of the Pharaoh's mood.

Nevertheless, this made no difference to the construction schedule. The people arrived each day for work but their performance deteriorated and the pyramid construction fell further behind schedule.

The Pharaoh responded in the only way he knew. He consulted his advisers again but they could offer nothing new and half the team were dismissed. Bringing in new blood would, he believed, make a difference. But he was wrong, and soon the pyramid building journey had reached a near standstill.

Matters came to a head when the Pharaoh contracted a serious virus, and became convinced he was going to die. If he did, he would be unable to enter the New World. He had no pyramid. He would go down in history as the unachieving Pharaoh.

For days he drifted in and out of consciousness, constantly experiencing nightmares involving his rejection at the door of the god Osiris. She refused to let him enter her kingdom. He was a failure.

When his fever eventually subsided he woke up and realised that enough was enough.

He would have to pay Prem a visit.

The First Meeting

When the Pharaoh announced to his officials that he was going to meet up with Prem, there was a huge sigh of relief. Like the Pharaoh, they didn't fully understand what one individual could bring to the journey, but if he were able to take the pressure off them his contribution would be worthwhile.

In advance of the meeting, the Pharaoh spent some time investigating the Sage's background. Although based predominantly in Egypt, he was born in another land, and had spent many years abroad. Prem's education was very different from the Egyptian tradition and was based on knowledge, skill and experience amassed over many years. Trial and error played a key part in his early work. Learning from mistakes shaped his thinking. Learning from books did not.

Rather than summon Prem to the Royal Palace, the Pharaoh thought a visit to his home would enable him to gain a better understanding of the man. Arrangements were made and, on arrival at Prem's house, Smendes was taken into the main reception room. Against the walls were seemingly countless shelves containing mountainous heaps of papyrus scrolls.

Smendes picked up several scrolls at random. Many were in languages foreign to him, but all those written in the hieroglyphs that he could read seemed to be votes of thanks and letters of gratitude to the Sage. The Pharaoh heard a cough and turned to see Prem bowing from the doorway. "You honour me with your visit, sir."

Smendes nodded his head in acknowledgement,

Prem invited the Pharaoh into his office at the back of the house. The walls again were covered, this time with many framed inscriptions making mention of 'the journey'. There was one large frame in particular, which made reference to 'the formula'. Even after he had looked at much that was on display, the Pharaoh still couldn't work out what Prem's vocation was.

"What do you actually do?" asked the Pharaoh, pointing to the displays on each wall. "These are all fascinating but what do they mean?"

Prem thought for a few moments.

"All of my clients are on a journey of some sort: a journey of discovery, a journey of change, a journey of creation, a journey of personal growth. My job is to help and guide them throughout their journey and to ensure that they reach their chosen destination on time."

The Pharaoh was none the wiser and asked him to elaborate.

Prem continued, "The people I work with have an idea, a dream or an ambition that they would like to realise. They surround themselves with other people who they trust will support them in their endeavour. They are ambitious, positive and energetic. Unfortunately, on their journey they encounter difficulties, challenges and frustrations that could prevent them from reaching their ultimate destination. My role is to help them minimise the difficulties, avoid many of the frustrations and overcome the challenges on the journey.

"In your case you are striving to construct the perfect pyramid. I also know that you are behind schedule and you face many challenges at the moment. You will face many more in the future."

The Pharaoh placed his hands on the Sage's shoulders in an almost fraternal gesture: "Will you build the pyramid for me?"

"That I cannot do, sir, but what I will do is work with you to make sure that it happens."

"What good is that to me?" demanded the Pharaoh. "I have nearly twenty-thousand people already working with me to build the pyramid. Another person will make no difference."

"I beg to differ," was the reply. "First of all the people are not working with you, they merely give the appearance of doing so; they are unsure of your motives. There are rumours of future war and many of the people don't like you." He continued, "They are working on the pyramid construction not because they want to but out of a sense of duty. Secondly, I can make a difference to the construction but only if you believe that I can. You have already asked your people to take a leap of faith in you. I'm asking you to do the same. Have faith in my ability to help you realise your dream."

Prem's frankness staggered the Pharaoh. He was not used to such forthright opinions and, worse, felt wounded by these insights. He could only respond with anger.

"Then you too can work on the pyramid out of a sense of duty! I am commanding you to help me. I am the Pharaoh, the supreme ruler of Egypt. There will be no leap of faith. I expect you to help."

The Sage gestured to a nearby couch, and when the Pharaoh refused his invitation to sit, he sat down instead. "Forgive my directness, but I imagine that the way you have just spoken to me is the same manner in which you have spoken to your managers and advisers. It is little wonder that morale in the kingdom is so low."

He continued, "In truth, I am not an Egyptian subject. I am not obligated to help you in the building of your pyramid, although I would like to do so. In the same way, I helped your mother because I wanted to, not because I was forced. There is a marked difference."

Despite his anger, the Pharaoh had to admit that Prem had a point. Perhaps, he thought, the people of Egypt were really working on the pyramid because they had to and not because they wanted to. Perhaps this was the main reason why the construction was behind schedule.

"Your mother and I had a fine relationship. We achieved a lot and in our time together, she never once commanded me to help her. It was an honour and a privilege to work with her."

"Very well," said the Pharaoh, his temper cooling slightly. "When you said 'have faith in you', what did you mean?"

"I know the six stages to building the pyramid. I don't mean the six phases to the construction of the pyramid. I mean the formula; the six stages designed to ensure that the pyramid-building journey is completed satisfactorily and on time. Trust me, and I will share my experience, built up over years, with you."

Prem continued, "For the journey to be completed successfully, we have to understand and respect each other's roles. You know more about pyramid building than I could ever dream of and, since you were a child, you have been groomed to be Pharaoh.

"I have no right to tell you how your pyramid should be built. That is your responsibility. I also don't have a right to comment on the quality of your advisers. They are your appointments, and in time you will find out whether they are right for the journey.

"But I do know that you have made the best possible decisions on your journey so far based on the information you have to hand. You should be pleased with what you have achieved to date, but your journey is only beginning."

The Pharaoh was beginning to warm to this strange and outspoken man.

"Have a look at this." He guided the Pharaoh over to a framed inscription on the wall. It read:

'You don't know what you don't know!'

"Any Pharaoh is only as good as the knowledge, experience and skill gained over their years as ruler of their kingdom. You yourself had a great upbringing. You were surrounded by accomplished scribes and scholars who taught you just about everything you know. Your mother also taught you a great deal. But you still don't know what you don't know!

"Tomorrow you will learn more, and the next day and the next. Adopting the philosophy 'you don't know what you don't know' will be critical to the relationship we have together and the success we enjoy on the pyramid-building journey."

"The philosophy applies equally to me," Prem continued. "The six stages that make up the formula have been developed over many years, working with many people. I can provide you with the best possible advice I am able to offer you today. But I learn something new each day. I am then able to keep adding something more valuable to the formula, which means everyone then benefits."

The Pharaoh smiled and suggested that they forget their bad start and begin again. Prem agreed.

"How often would we meet and work together? Will you tell me the six stages today? How will I know that they are working?" The Pharaoh had so many questions to ask and was impatient to get started on the journey.

Prem replied that the six stages would be revealed over the lifespan of the journey and that the outcomes of each stage would be clearly visible.

"Why don't you just tell me the six stages now?" persisted the Pharaoh. "It would save a lot of time, and would enable me to bring the journey back on schedule."

Prem smiled and pointed again to the inscription, 'You don't know what you don't know' on the wall.

The Pharaoh conceded the point, but he wasn't quite finished. He needed some reassurance that the True Scholar was capable of this huge undertaking. He was yet to pass the Pharaoh's personal test and so, not unreasonably, the King asked for some evidence of his record of achievement.

"You must concede that I will be announcing your input to my advisers, and they will need to be convinced that you understand the issues that we currently face," said the Pharaoh. "Very few of them know you and none that I know of have worked with you."

The Pharaoh had made a valid point. For the journey to be successful, Prem would need the support of the Pharaoh's team of advisers and managers. Alienating them at the beginning of the journey would not be a good start.

He had to give the Pharaoh something to take back to his team. He opened a chest and gave Smendes a sealed document. "Will this help?" he asked.

The Pharaoh opened the document. It was titled 'The challenges faced on the pyramid-building journey'. It listed a number of factors that had to be addressed by the Pharaoh and the people of Egypt if the journey was to be completed successfully.

"Over the years, I have learned that building a pyramid involves a number of challenges, all of which test the dedication of everyone involved.

"To fund construction, trade will have to be maintained and, throughout the years of the construction journey, improvements in efficiency will have to be made. The people working on the project will also need constant training to develop skills, perhaps helped by people not themselves involved in the work.

"There will be high and low points on the journey and, to compensate for these, communication with the workforce is vital."

He looked directly into the Pharaoh's eyes.

"Two of your biggest challenges, sir, will be to gain the support of your people to the project, and to manage the change needed to complete the journey, a journey that will affect everyone in the land."

"Understand these challenges, produce a plan accordingly and success will be yours."

The Pharaoh was impressed. He clasped Prem's hand and thanked him for his time. On the way back to the palace, Smendes was in a reflective mood. Prem had indicated that he would challenge his thinking, his ideas, values and the purpose of the journey. As the Pharaoh, the supreme ruler of Egypt and the most important man in the kingdom, he didn't like the sound of that.

But he also knew there was no other scholar experienced or specialised in the completion of journeys.

When he arrived back at the palace he made his decision. Orders were given to despatch a servant to the Sage's house with the message 'I will see you in two days to begin the journey. I look forward to learning about the formula.'

Lessons from the Journey

- Every leader wishes to build his unique pyramid. Most leaders are clear about their vision

- Embarking on the journey often involves taking a leap of faith in the leader at the head of the organisation. Instilling confidence is the leader's number one priority

- The greater the leader's knowledge of the journey, the greater the chance of success

- Just because leaders have operated in a certain way in the past does not mean they have to operate in the same way in the future

- The biggest challenge for any leader is not the plan itself, but the execution of the plan

- New leaders who rush to build without a plan run the risk of their own credibility coming into question and under scrutiny

- The direction set by the leader at the start of the journey and the impression they create will shape what comes next

- Each journey is unique with its own set of challenges, milestones and barriers to success designed to test the capability of the leader

- It's often not until they are lost that leaders realise they do not possess all the answers to all the problems. They need advice and support

- Having the title of 'leader' doesn't guarantee support and commitment from others

- Success will require leaders to focus on six key strategic and operational areas on the journey

- The growth journey is one of the most exciting, challenging and rewarding experiences any leader can have

- Navigating the journey will require the use of a performance framework to keep people 'on track'

Post-Coronation

"Everyone dreams of being part of something special!"

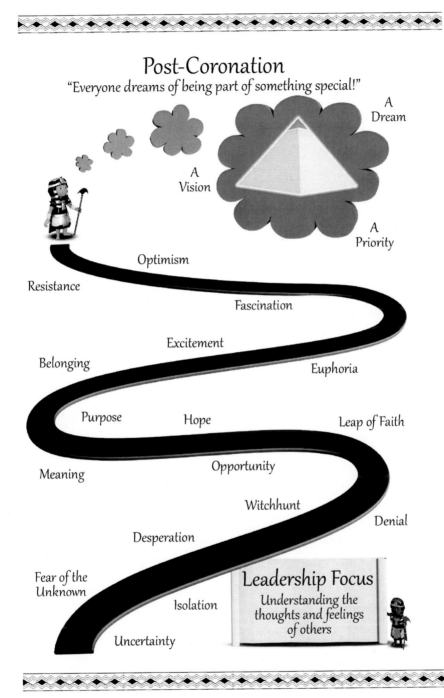

A Dream

A Vision

A Priority

Optimism

Resistance

Fascination

Excitement

Belonging

Euphoria

Purpose

Hope

Leap of Faith

Meaning

Opportunity

Witchhunt

Denial

Desperation

Fear of the Unknown

Isolation

Uncertainty

Leadership Focus
Understanding the thoughts and feelings of others

Laying New Foundations

"The avenue to the temple is identifying what lies beneath"

The Pharaoh announced to his senior team of advisers that Prem would be helping them to build the perfect pyramid.

"Be assured that he will not interfere in the day-to-day construction of the pyramid," said Smendes, "or for that matter have anything to do with the jobs of the senior team of advisers." This helped allay some fears, although others existed.

"How do we know if he understands the problems we face as a team?" asked the Trade Ambassador. "He's not even Egyptian. How could he possibly understand the importance of the pyramid to us?"

The Pharaoh thought for a few moments.

"Consider this. If we always do what we always did, we will always get what we always got!" The team listened to the words and tried to make sense of them.

"We are two years behind schedule and you are unable to demonstrate to me how we can avoid disaster. The reality is," continued the Pharaoh, "if we always do what we always did, we will always get what we always got. In this instance, it means low productivity from our people resulting in an unfinished pyramid. I can't allow this to happen, and that's why we will be involving the Sage in the project."

The team couldn't disagree with the Pharaoh's logic. They knew that something had to change, but they didn't know what.

"He also gave me this," said the Pharaoh, producing the document presented to him, highlighting the main challenges faced by the team on their pyramid-building journey. The document was passed around the table.

Every member of the team read it and each was astonished by its insight.

"I think that's enough proof. I expect everyone here today to support the Sage. Work with him begins next week," ordered the Pharaoh.

At the agreed date and time, Prem arrived at the Royal Palace for his first formal session with the Pharaoh. In advance of the meeting, Prem had asked the Pharaoh to prepare a detailed report of the pyramid project to date. The presentation took up the first part of the morning and included the composition of the Pharaoh's team, the current position of the journey in relation to the planned schedule, and the problems and difficulties faced to date. The remainder of the morning was spent meeting each member of the team.

When they met for their midday meal, The Pharaoh asked about the formula and what would be involved.

"Stage one of the formula is about research," Prem replied. "It is the most important stage in the overall process and where most journeys go wrong, at the beginning."

He related the stage to the Pharaoh's own pyramid-construction process, stressing the importance of laying the correct foundations. Stage one of the formula would involve the development of a solid base, one that would enable the five other stages to be carried out successfully in the future.

Prem went on to explain the three reasons why journeys fail at the beginning.

1. The reasons for embarking on the journey are not instantly clear to the people who are asked to join it. That means that they join for the wrong reasons, sometimes out of a sense of duty, because it is expected or perhaps because they have been forced to.

2. The challenges likely to be encountered throughout the journey are very rarely identified in advance of the start and communicated to the people. When problems then occurred, people were not prepared and would start to mistrust the leaders. "People don't like surprises. They prefer to know the good and the bad parts of the journey from the outset, so that they can prepare themselves," said Prem.

3. The journey is not communicated and presented in a way in which the people can imagine what it will look like and mean to them. The stronger and more compelling his vision was, the easier it would be to enlist and sustain support, and focus his people on the construction of the pyramid.

Prem asked the Pharaoh to recollect how the journey had been communicated to his people, but before Smendes could respond, Prem rose to his feet and, arms spread wide, gave his version of the proclamation. "The Pharaoh has announced that we are going on a new journey to build the perfect pyramid. It is your duty to support him as your new ruler. Enlist right away and ensure that he is ready to meet the sun-god Osiris when his time comes to leave the Old World."

"And what's wrong with that?" asked the Pharaoh.

"Well let's consider those words," replied Prem. "we are going…it is your duty…enlist now…ensure…"

"How do you think your people felt when they heard your proclamation, particularly when they were yet to meet you?"

The Pharaoh understood the point he was making. It was too direct and aggressive. It also lacked the personal touch; it was selfish and focused totally on his needs. It was an instruction, a command, rather than a vision which his people could be part of.

Prem explained to the Pharaoh that his announcement to his people was well meaning, but that he had made a common mistake in not involving his people in the planning stage. This was why he received such a poor response to his call to action.

Prem cheerfully assured him that all was not lost, and that they would soon make up lost ground.

To obtain support from his people on the journey he would have to carry out additional work with his team, based on the three reasons for failure discussed earlier.

The Pharaoh was asked to:

1.   Agree what Prem called the imperatives for growth, the main reasons why the people of Egypt should embark on the Pharaoh's journey. This information would be used to earn commitment from his people, both now and in the future, to the journey.

2.   Identify the anticipated challenges and hurdles that the Pharaoh and his team were likely to encounter throughout the journey.

3.   Produce a vision of what the journey would look like for everyone in Egypt. In conjunction with the imperatives for growth, the vision would be used to inspire people to support the journey, play a personal part in the realisation of the Pharaoh's dream and overcome any challenges and obstacles.

Prem told the Pharaoh that the outcomes produced from the work would form part of what he called the 'Journey Map', which would be used by the Pharaoh's team of advisers and managers to lead and guide the people over the time-span of the pyramid construction.

Prem returned to the palace a few weeks later to discover that his team had worked long and hard and had produced three outstanding pieces of work. The Pharaoh handed the three documents to the Sage.

He opened and read the first document, the 'Imperatives for growth'. The team had highlighted six main reasons why they were embarking on the journey.

REASONS FOR EMBARKING ON THE JOURNEY

The Pharaoh's Journey into the Afterlife

The most important reason for us embarking on the journey. Our Pharaoh is a god. Only he can represent us and ensure that our dreams and ambitions can become a reality. Helping him on his journey into the Afterlife will benefit us all.

The Passage to Heaven for All Egyptian People

Our Pharaoh will talk to the sun-god Osiris on our behalf and will ensure that, when it is time, our passage to heaven will have been prepared for us.

Egypt's Status in the World

We pride ourselves in being the wealthiest country in the world. Everyone playing his or her personal part on the Pharaoh's journey will ensure that our status will remain for generations to come.

Threats

Given an opportunity, our enemies will attempt to steal our riches and rob us of our future. Building the Pharaoh's pyramid will send a message to them that we are ready and willing to defend our nation.

Future Wealth and Security

Building the pyramid and supporting the Pharaoh on his journey will ensure future wealth and security for our people.

Approval from the Gods

We have a duty to worship our gods, support our Pharaoh and retain their approval of our wishes and dreams for our great kingdom.

Prem was impressed with the document, particularly the simplicity of the six statements.

The second document was an amended version of the 'Challenges' document that had been presented to the Pharaoh. In total it included twelve challenges that the team of advisers believed summarised the demands that would be placed on them.

CHALLENGES ON THE JOURNEY

🔲 *Sustaining and improving trade with other nations*

🔲 *Improving productivity and efficiency throughout the pyramid construction*

🔲 *Managing the Pharaoh's journey and the necessary change required*

🔲 *Sustaining the Egyptian people's focus throughout the journey*

🔲 *Recruiting new talent and expertise when the time was right*

🔲 *Developing and promoting the benefits of the pyramid*

🔲 *Retaining existing talent within the Kingdom of Egypt*

🔲 *Funding the resources required to succeed on the journey*

🔲 *Developing new building systems and processes*

🔲 *Communicating the journey's progress to everyone in the kingdom*

🔲 *Improving the knowledge and skills of the Egyptian people*

🔲 *Gaining widespread support to the Pharaoh's journey to the New World*

Finally, the True Scholar opened the 'Vision' document, the most important element of the Journey Map. He read it several times. It began by saying:

Our overall 'vision' is to create for our Pharaoh and the Kingdom of Egypt a monument, which will transport our King to the heavens above where he will meet our sun-god Osiris in the New World. Our plan is to construct the perfect pyramid. This will be a structure unlike any built beforehand…..It will be a truly impressive monument…Future generations of people in Egypt and around the world will visit the Pharaoh's tomb and will marvel at the ingenuity and workmanship.

It mentioned that:

Every person in Egypt will play their part in its construction – at the quarry, on the pyramid site, in the deserts, the villages and by the banks of the Nile.

And that:

The pyramid will be known throughout the kingdom as a place to worship and a place at which to feel proud to be an Egyptian.

It concluded by saying:

The culmination of the support by the people of Egypt will be the completion of the perfect pyramid ahead of the agreed schedule. The measurement of the nation's success will be the successful transportation of our Pharaoh from the Old World to the New World and the pride and satisfaction from each Egyptian, knowing that they played their part in his onward journey.

Prem put the three documents down on the table in front of him and congratulated the Pharaoh on a magnificent piece of work. The Pharaoh smiled and for the first time on his pyramid-building journey felt a real sense of achievement. He knew there was a lot to do and this was only the start, but what a start.

"So where do we go from here?" asked the Pharaoh.

The Sage asked the Pharaoh to go back to his team, congratulate them on their outstanding work and to test the three documents with a few groups of people that Prem had in mind. The Pharaoh was asked if he would meet again in a month's time to discuss his findings.

When Prem arrived at the palace some weeks later the Pharaoh was ready to greet him at the gates, wearing a broad smile.

"I see, sir," said the Sage "that you are eager to tell me something."

The Pharaoh began by telling Prem how pleased his team of advisers and officials were with the report on their work in completing the 'Imperatives for growth', 'Challenges' and 'Vision' documents. Since then, he noticed how they had grown in stature, pride and self-confidence.

The presentation of the documents to the Egyptian people had also gone well. Prem had identified twenty teams across the construction process to be part of a communication and discussion exercise, chaired by chosen officials.

The exercises were designed to gauge the initial reaction from a sample of the Egyptian public to the work and, at the same time, to learn lessons that could be used for the future. It was pointless, explained Prem, to launch the work to all of the Egyptian people without first testing it. The Pharaoh had agreed with his approach.

The Pharaoh began to outline to Prem the people's reaction to the three documents presented to them. He began with the 'Imperatives for growth', the six reasons why they should embark on the Pharaoh's journey.

Many people in the kingdom had been tired of having the importance of the Pharaoh's journey drummed into them. To them it wasn't news anymore and so, every time they heard a supervisor talk about their duty, they didn't really listen. They were also carrying pre-conceptions – whether good or bad – of the journey.

When, however, they were presented with the full document, they began to realise its significance, particularly the reference to Egypt's status, its future wealth, security and the commitment to their children's future. Now that they had a better understanding of the reasons for the journey, they viewed the construction in a very different light. Clearly, to gain the support of his people to his journey, the Pharaoh would have to spend a lot of time communicating his vision.

The Pharaoh then discussed the reaction to the 'Challenges' document. He explained that not everyone was initially interested in it. Many people could, however, see that the challenges related to every one of their job functions on the journey and were honest enough to say that they had never given much thought to the bigger picture within the country. It had become clear that, on the journey, Smendes would have to be realistic. Not everyone, he admitted, was at the same level of commitment.

Prem acknowledged the point but told the Pharaoh not to be concerned at the moment with the differing reactions. The fact that his team had identified the challenges and were now presenting them to the people would reap benefits later on.

The Pharaoh did acknowledge that the people seemed to have renewed confidence in the leaders and advisers involved in the test sessions. He put it down to the open and honest way in which the documents were presented.

Smendes then moved onto the 'Vision' document. He explained that everyone received this part of the session remarkably well. There were no exceptions; the people were enthused and inspired by the presentation of the Pharaoh's vision.

For the first time in his reign, the people had a clear idea of what the Pharaoh wanted to achieve in the kingdom. They also liked the tone and the style of the 'Vision' document. They constantly referred to many of the words and phrases such as...the perfect pyramid...unlike any before... truly impressive...expertise of the people...will marvel and admire...feel proud to be an Egyptian...played their part in his onward journey. They also commented that it looked like a vision that had been created by the people for the people.

The Pharaoh put his notes down and beamed with delight.

"Wonderful news," said Prem, "and richly deserved. Your team put a lot of work into the documents."

The Pharaoh had not finished. He said that he appreciated how the three documents helped his team of advisers and managers communicate the journey to the twenty teams. He noticed that many of them were already showing signs of being true leaders. There was also a consistency of message across the team, which he felt was missing previously from the journey.

"However, I do still have several issues," continued Smendes. He explained that, even allowing for the completion of the good work by his team in the past few weeks, he couldn't escape the fact that the pyramid was still seriously behind schedule. He felt that it was time to present the 'Imperatives', 'Challenges' and 'Vision' documents to the remainder of the people within his kingdom. Energy levels and enthusiasm had increased in virtually every team involved in the test. Surely by announcing the information contained in the documents, the pyramid construction would be brought back on schedule.

He had also noticed that several members of his team were beginning to ask how the vision would be achieved. They believed in the sentiment behind it, but felt the detail of its delivery was missing.

Prem acknowledged these issues but suggested to the Pharaoh that there was no merit in announcing the documents to the remainder of the kingdom. Not yet anyway.

"Remember that what you have just completed is a test, no more than that. As a result, you have been able to gauge the reaction of some of your people to your first piece of work. You have also learned a great deal about their reaction to its presentation. But now is not the time to offer it to everyone in the kingdom. Not until we have addressed the challenge you just mentioned to me, the detail missing in the achievement of the vision."

The Pharaoh looked despondent. He was a man in a hurry and he wasn't used to being kept waiting. However, Prem told him that rather than being despondent, he should celebrate success so far – the completion of stage one.

Lessons from the Journey

🔖   The Research stage focuses on the size of the opportunity for everyone likely to be involved on the journey

🔖   It also describes the leadership approach to inspiring others to sign up to the journey and help build the pyramid

🔖   The reasons for embarking on the journey – the imperatives for growth – will remove any cynicism people may have about the future. It will enable them to answer the question, "What's in it for me?"

🔖   Imperatives for growth will include survival, new markets, growth potential and status, and personal imperatives such as a sense of adventure, personal growth, fulfilment, pride and being part of a special cause!

🔖   The vision should be simple, ambitious, compelling and inspiring. That will make it easier to attract, recruit and retain people on the journey

🔖   Understand the difference between a vision and an instruction

🔖   The vision highlights the destination, purpose, workplace experience, challenges involved, support issued and the measure of success

🔖   Involving people in the development of the vision guarantees a high level of commitment at the start of the journey

🔖   When times are tough, 'the size of the opportunity' will galvanise individuals and keep people focused on the destination

🔖   Remember people don't like surprises. Identify and communicate challenges likely to be facing them at the outset and let them decide if they wish to join the journey

🔖   Everyone wants to be part of something special

🔖   The imperatives, challenges and vision form part of the journey map

🔖   Navigating the journey will require a clear understanding of the landscape

Stage One: Research

"The role of the leader is to create a kingdom
that others want to be a part of"

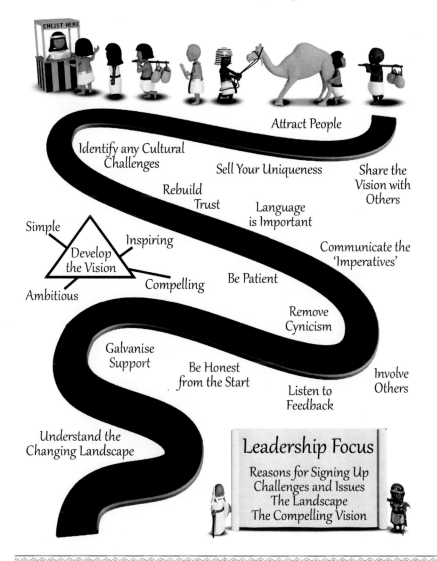

Attract People

Identify any Cultural
Challenges

Sell Your Uniqueness

Share the
Vision with
Others

Rebuild
Trust

Language
is Important

Simple

Inspiring

Develop
the Vision

Communicate the
'Imperatives'

Ambitious

Compelling

Be Patient

Remove
Cynicism

Galvanise
Support

Be Honest
from the Start

Involve
Others

Listen to
Feedback

Understand the
Changing Landscape

Leadership Focus

Reasons for Signing Up
Challenges and Issues
The Landscape
The Compelling Vision

The Way Ahead

"The papyrus will negotiate the perils through the hall of two truths"

Stage two, which Prem called Strategy, began. Prem had used the word 'map' several times in stage one of the journey. Stage two, he told Smendes, would involve its development and production. He went on to explain that the map was a manuscript discussed, developed and produced by the Pharaoh and his team of advisers.

It would be a simple document designed to announce the journey to the people of Egypt. It would include the approach that would be taken throughout the journey and would encompass the previous work carried out by the team: the 'Imperatives for growth', the 'Challenges' and the Pharaoh's 'Vision'. It would take approximately two months to complete and would include the missing detail that the Pharaoh had referred to earlier on.

Every person in the kingdom, and Egypt's trading partners, would receive a copy describing, in simple terms, the Pharaoh's journey.

The Pharaoh was, however, unhappy about revealing the contents of the 'Journey Map' and worried about it falling into wrong hands. It could be copied and it would contain the secret formula.

Prem listened to the Pharaoh's concerns.

"First let me explain why we need the map and then I will address your fears and concerns about its production," he responded.

"You will need the commitment of twenty-thousand people scattered over all forty-two provinces to complete the pyramid on time. The task of communicating your vision and obtaining the support you need will be as enormous an undertaking as the physical construction of the pyramid."

The Pharaoh agreed.

"Consider this, if you will. With an average of one adviser, manager or supervisor to fifty people on the construction project, we have to rely on four-hundred people to present the message to them. That is a huge exercise in communication. It also doesn't take into account the millions of people in the country who influence each other today, tomorrow and the next day. They also need to be involved. You can see that the map is a vital tool for us if we are to be successful on the journey."

The Pharaoh, again, agreed.

"The map, to us and the people of Egypt, will be as important a tool of support as are the sledges that transport the stone blocks or the chisels the stone masons use. Without the map, we would be unable to function."

"I understand your concern about your enemies obtaining the map, but you really have nothing to worry about," Prem continued.

"Let's assume that one of your enemies got hold of the three pieces of work that you and your team have just completed. How could it possibly help them?" It is one thing to know what the formula is, but it is another to know how to use it. The secrets explain the process, but it's the hearts and minds of the people that make the journey happen."

The Pharaoh relaxed, as he could relate to the explanation given. He knew about pyramid building and matters of state but that hadn't saved him from the predicament he was in. If the hearts and minds of the people weren't with you, you had no chance of being successful, he thought.

Sensing that the Pharaoh was happy to continue, Prem began to explain the missing detail that was required for the map to be completed. The first thing he asked the Pharaoh to consider was what he called the 'Critical success factors'.

The Pharaoh was asked to identify the main areas of focus that would have to be worked on to ensure that the journey to completion was carried out successfully – in other words, the factors critical to success. Prem gave him a few examples such as the security of the kingdom and the availability of food and water as a starting point.

He explained that if these two factors and others that his team would identify were not achieved, then the construction process would end in disaster and the vision would not be realised.

The Pharaoh thought this straightforward enough. He and his team would often have meetings to discuss what was needed to ensure that the pyramid would be completed. It was just a matter of pulling the information together at their next session.

Then Prem asked him to discuss, agree and produce with his team what he called a 'culture statement'. He explained that for any journey to be completed successfully, the behaviour of the people on the journey had to be appropriate to the needs of all the participants.

It was the responsibility of the Pharaoh and his team of advisers to document the behaviours they would like to see demonstrated by everyone in the kingdom throughout the building of the pyramid.

The next day the Pharaoh began the work with his team of officials and advisers. Four weeks later, he let Prem know that he was ready to meet up again. He had completed the two tasks and was ready to present them.

When they met up, the 'Critical success factors' were presented. These comprised eleven areas of focus that, if supported by the people within the kingdom, would guarantee the realisation of the Pharaoh's vision. Under each factor the Pharaoh's team had included an objective to clarify what was to be achieved. They included the following:

CRITICAL SUCCESS FACTORS

1. Food and Water Supply
'To provide the people of Egypt with a continuous supply of food and water'

2. Unique Egyptian Culture
'To maintain the unique traditions of the Egyptian culture throughout all aspects of our society'

3. Security of the Kingdom
'To maintain the security of the country against our neighbouring states and potential enemies'

4. Future Trade
'To increase the level of trade enjoyed with other countries'

5. Wealth and Prosperity
'To ensure that the kingdom retains its status as the wealthiest nation in the world'

6. Health and Safety
'To provide the necessary resources and support required to ensure the continued well being of the Egyptian people'

7. Landmark Achievement
'To ensure that all agreed landmarks are achieved in the building of the pyramid'

8. Support of the Gods
'To make every effort to worship and engage the support of our gods'

9. Resources
'To provide the necessary tools, equipment and resources throughout the pyramid-building journey'

10. Attention to Detail
'To maintain high standards of work throughout all aspects of the pyramid construction'

11. Transport
'To produce routes that will enable the efficient transportation of goods and materials throughout the kingdom'

The Pharaoh then presented the second document containing the culture statement, which read:

CULTURE STATEMENT

We expect our people to:

🔯 *Play an active part in ensuring the Pharaoh's onward journey into the New World*

🔯 *Understand fully the component parts of the Pharaoh's map*

🔯 *Encourage and respect the contribution that others can make to the journey*

🔯 *Offer ideas and suggestions on how the Pharaoh's pyramid can be constructed successfully*

🔯 *Take time out to worship and thank the gods for their support*

🔯 *Celebrate success at each stage of the pyramid's construction*

🔯 *Work hard on the journey and make the most of leisure, family and friends*

🔯 *Encourage others to make a contribution to the Pharaoh's journey*

🔯 *Make the necessary plans for their own journey into the New World*

🔯 *Be loyal to the Pharaoh and to the Kingdom of Egypt*

'Have the wisdom to abandon the values of a time that has passed and pick out the constituents of the future. An environment must be suited to an age and men to their environment.

Prem was once again impressed with the team's work and announced to the Pharaoh that stage two of the journey had successfully been completed.

Lessons from the Journey

- The Strategy stage focuses on the production of the journey map

- It also describes the leadership approach to communicating how the vision will be achieved on the journey

- Navigating the right path on the journey requires a map that must be simple and easy to understand.

- Critical success factors, objectives and culture form part of the journey map

- The critical success factors include areas of focus important to the completion of the journey

- Each factor should be linked to the development of an objective important to explaining to others how the pyramid will be built

- The culture statement represents the behaviour expected by everyone throughout the time-span of the journey

- The map is a powerful and visual plan highlighting how the pyramid will be built and bringing the journey to life. (A picture is worth a thousand words)

- The production process helps leaders instill confidence and plan the resources required to successfully complete the journey

- A journey without a map will end up with people in the middle of the desert – not where you want to be

- The map can be used to evaluate the progress being made at any given time on the journey

- The map is used as a support tool for leaders to manage others on the journey, no matter when they sign up

- Navigating the journey will require the need to adjust the course as necessary while staying focused on the destination

Stage Two: Strategy

"The role of the leader is to demonstrate to everyone connected with the kingdom, how the ambitious plan will be realised"

Demonstrate the
Way Forward to
Everyone

Offer Direction and Support

Address Questions
Raised By People

Simple is Powerful

Identify Areas of
Strategic Focus

Reinforce
the Vision

Demonstrate Link
with Each Role

Identify Important
Behaviours Required

Understand
the Rules of the
Journey

Develop Leadership
Confidence

Produce a
Route Map

Involve Others
in the Strategy

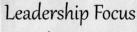

Leadership Focus

Critical Success Factors
Culture & Values
Link with Performance
Blueprint for Success

Obtaining Commitment

*"Earn commitment and you will steer them on the
journey to the promised land"*

Smendes was now ready to begin announcing the Journey Map to his
people. He was in a hurry; his pyramid was still behind schedule and he
feared that his death would come before he had an opportunity to prepare
for the New World.

He travelled to Prem's home fully expecting to be able to proceed and
communicate the map to the people of Egypt. Prem had other ideas.

He explained to the Pharaoh that although he and his team had produced
five pieces of outstanding work, there was a final component missing. The
Pharaoh was baffled by Prem's reluctance to communicate the map but
reminded himself that, "You don't know what you don't know."

Prem explained the principles behind what he called the power of
engagement, stage three of the journey. These principles were relevant to
all journeys and related to the level of commitment of the people to actively
play their part in their completion. He explained that when a new journey is
announced, its initial success is based on how it is communicated. People
respond to the idea of the journey in three different ways.

One group of people will support it from the outset because they believe in
the Pharaoh and the purpose of the journey. Prem called these people 'the
great advocates' or 'the true believers'.

The second group, he explained, will do the exact opposite. They will
dig their heels in and be obstructive to the reasons for the journey and
their expected contribution. They often carry negative experiences from
previous journeys, normally as a result of being let down through false or
broken promises or more usually, poor leadership. The True Scholar called
these people 'the cautious', or 'the undecided'.

The third group, he continued, are caught in the middle. They are unsure whether to join the group of great advocates or perhaps join up with the cautious. They need to be convinced of the importance of the journey. The great majority of people at the beginning of any journey are in this group. Prem called them 'the trusting', for they base their commitment to the journey on trust.

The Pharaoh agreed with the groupings and saw that they applied to everyone in the kingdom. He recalled noticing them within his first team of advisers and managers at the beginning of the journey.

Prem went on to explain that, for the journey to be successful with twenty thousand people committed to the vision, he had to first of all increase the number of leaders engaged in the journey. Twenty-five advisers and managers would not be enough to influence twenty-thousand people. The Sage's plan was to develop a team of what he called 'Cultural Architects'. People who would communicate, influence and engage the people of Egypt. Prem explained that the more Cultural Architects there were, the more people would commit to the journey.

The Cultural Architects would initially be recruited from the first group, the great advocates, and their strategy would be to influence the middle group, the trusting, by handling their fears and concerns. Prem explained, "The success you will enjoy on the journey will relate directly to the level of engagement by your people."

Prem moved onto his next point. He said that one of the biggest mistakes leaders make when announcing a journey is presenting their plans without first involving their people in the production of their map.

"In order for you to succeed in engaging your people, you are going to have to test again the work carried out by your team, this time in a different way and with a different group of people."

Prem explained to the Pharaoh that this test would be unlike the previous ones where they announced to the twenty teams the three documents and then gauged their reactions. This time he was asking the advisers and managers to go out to the kingdom and, as Prem put it, "give the people a good listening to!"

"What do you mean?" asked the Pharaoh.

"Well, simply put, rather than doing what most advisers and managers do, which is to give their people a good talking to, I need you to do the exact opposite."

He explained to the Pharaoh that he needed to carry out a survey of his people's thoughts and views on himself, his team of advisers, the way in which the construction of the pyramid was being carried out and also how the kingdom was being run. He could see the Pharaoh turning pale at his advice.

"I assume that you jest!" said the Pharaoh, "Why would I invite the people to criticise? What is the point of that?" There was a sudden and very real tension emanating from Smendes.

"If you want to survive the sting of a scorpion, you must first suck out the poison," said Prem. "If poison exists in the hearts and minds of the people, we need to be made aware of it, and then we need to remove it. Unless you can think of an alternative way of engaging your people, then we have to carry out the survey."

The Pharaoh considered for a few moments, but he couldn't think of an alternative method.

"As you wish," he said, reluctantly.

Prem explained that he would personally manage the survey with the support of the Pharaoh and his team. In the past, Pharaohs had tried to carry out surveys themselves, and had always failed. Prem had learnt that when the people are unsure of the purpose of the journey, they were unlikely to support the survey process. Only an outsider could begin the process of developing trust on any journey.

The Sage would involve three-thousand people who were already participating in the current construction of the pyramid, and a further two-thousand from the forty-two provinces that made up the kingdom.

He would organise a team of one hundred Cultural Architects to meet the people, and ask them for their thoughts on ten areas:

1. The overall management of the kingdom

2. The pyramid construction process

3. Each person's working environment

4. Public services, including housing

5. Health and safety

6. Communication from the palace

7. Egyptian culture

8. Support to people on the journey

9. The leadership role of the Pharaoh

10. The role of the Pharaoh's high officials, advisers and managers

The whole exercise would take six weeks to complete. Prem would produce a confidential report from the feedback received and would make a presentation to the Pharaoh and his team at a pre-determined date.

Two weeks later, the Cultural Architects began the survey process with the Egyptian people. True to Prem's suggestion, they 'gave them a good listening to'. Four weeks later Prem, the Pharaoh and his team met to discuss the findings of the survey. The presentation lasted over two hours.

The summary of the findings included the following key points for consideration:

*   The Pharaoh was hardly ever visible outside the palace. Many of the people were yet to see him in public

*   The journey to build the pyramid was viewed as a duty to the kingdom. Very few people actually wanted to take part in it

- Anxiety existed about the security of the nation. Rumours had spread that Egypt was to go to war with Syria

- High officials in the palace were viewed as remote from the people and an unnecessary expense

- The kingdom overall was in a worse state than when his mother had reigned

- Certain food items were unavailable at the local markets

- Regarding the pyramid construction, sledges would often need replacing, tools had very short working lives and accidents occurred on a daily basis

- Communication across the kingdom was poor, resulting in a negative, whispering 'grapevine' existing in many of the villages

- Egyptians felt compromised on several parts of their culture, which was important to them. Attention to detail and pride in their work was replaced by the need to get the job done

- Egyptians were unsure of the Pharaoh's intentions for the kingdom

- Many people felt disconnected from the nation and no longer felt proud to be Egyptian

- The people were convinced that the gods were looking down on them and were unhappy with the Pharaoh, the people and the overall running of the kingdom

- Egyptians didn't feel recognised for their personal efforts on the journey

- Supervisors on construction sites were viewed as incapable of making decisions for themselves. They seemed to always refer back to the Pharaoh and his team, causing valuable loss of time

- It was believed that the construction of the pyramid would never meet its agreed schedule

- A number of people believed that the Pharaoh did not make best use of the talent which existed within the kingdom

- Suggestions to improve any part of the construction were hardly ever made. Egyptians didn't believe that the Pharaoh was interested in listening to them

To support the key points, Prem presented hundreds of specific pieces of anecdotal evidence reflecting the thoughts and views of the Egyptian people.

The presentation of the findings to the Pharaoh and his team of advisers ended in stunned silence. They couldn't quite believe the level of negativity in the kingdom, the lack of belief in the Pharaoh and his team, and the clear lack of commitment to the construction of the pyramid.

The simple fact was that they had worked very hard. They had tried to manage the mood of the nation by themselves. However, the harder they tried, the worse the situation got.

One or two members of the group didn't agree with the findings of the survey at all. It didn't seem to match their experience of how they saw the Kingdom of Egypt and the construction of the pyramid.

Prem explained to them that there was no benefit in denying the results. They had to respect the people's right to be heard and that their perception of the kingdom was their reality. The Pharaoh and his team would have to change their perceptions. Disagreeing with the survey findings wouldn't get them anywhere and wouldn't lead to changing the attitude of the population.

"Do you think that at home, on the sites, with their friends and as they play, the people are not voicing their concerns and displeasure? Of course, they are. It would be naïve of us to think they are not. The best thing that you have ever done is to carry out this exercise," he said.

"But how can you say that?" asked the Chief Treasurer. "I don't know about everyone else, but I have never felt so depressed."

Prem sensed it was time to raise the mood of the meeting. "Don't be despondent. You should be congratulated for your courage in carrying out this work. Remember, you and your Pharaoh have carried out this exercise for the first time in his reign."

"Giving the people an opportunity to speak requires a certain type of courage. You have all just demonstrated the mark of great leaders; the ability to truly involve your people in the journey."

The Sage then began to explain that the journey map could not be presented without the involvement of the people in the survey. By excluding their input, it would have been perceived as a manuscript produced by scholars for scholars.

They could now demonstrate to the people of Egypt that they had involved them in the journey development process. They had also received thousands of pieces of information, which they could use to test the validity and accuracy of the map.

Prem told the team that once the journey map addressed the concerns, fears and ambitions of the people, then it could be announced to the nation. In effect, what the people had done was to provide the checking mechanism for the journey.

When the team heard this their optimism returned.

Prem then tasked the team with cross-referencing the survey results with the contents of the journey map. He asked them to critically analyse the manuscript, to amend it where appropriate and to make it more relevant to the journey and the people's expectations. He also asked them to consider the following twelve questions.

1.   Have we taken into account the needs of the Pharaoh?

2.   Have we taken into account the needs of the high officials and leaders?

3.   Have we taken into account the needs of the people?

4.   Is the manuscript simple enough for everyone to understand?

5.   Is the vision compelling enough that people will be inspired by it?

6.   Are the reasons for embarking on the journey clear enough?

7.   Have we explained how the vision will be achieved?

8.   Are we able to demonstrate what each person's contribution to the journey will be?

9.   Is the size of the opportunity communicated in sufficient detail?

10. Is it a manuscript that we would be proud to present?

11. Will it help the Cultural Architects answer any questions from other people?

12. Will it engage the people of Egypt on the journey?

If they could answer 'yes' to all twelve questions then the journey map would be ready for presentation to the people of Egypt. Prem left them for the remainder of the day to complete the exercise. He rejoined them in the evening to be informed that the manuscript was ready.

Led by the Pharaoh's team, the nominated Cultural Architects could now introduce the map to the people of Egypt, 'cascading' it, as the Sage had put it.

Two months later, the process was complete. Everyone in the kingdom had heard about the contents of the map and had received a personal copy. Special copies were put on display throughout the villages and cities. Everyone in the kingdom was made aware of the pharaoh's journey and the importance of the journey map.

Feedback was immediate and beyond the Pharaoh's wildest dreams. The people of Egypt were delighted with the map and detail describing the Pharaoh's journey, and wanted to play their part in its completion. It was the talk of every city, village and town.

The Pharaoh met up with Prem to give him a progress report on the 'cascading' process. They were both delighted by the way in which the Cultural Architects had played their part. He told Prem of one specific observation he had made.

"If you don't understand the map, you can't then communicate it effectively to others. If you can't communicate it to others then it's because you are not referring to it yourself. If you are not referring to it, then it's unlikely you believe in it. Understanding and believing in its contents are critical to leading others."

Prem was delighted that the Pharaoh had picked up this observation. Belief in the contents of the map was indeed critical to leading others.

The Pharaoh also explained that he had learnt that, to the people of Egypt, the map represented a symbol of confidence in the journey. The symbol became more important the further the people were from the capital and the Pharaoh's Palace. He had learnt that, in the remote corners of the kingdom the map was even more important to engaging his people as they had less contact with officials, advisers or managers of the journey. He was also more reliant on the Cultural Architects to play their part in increasing the number of great advocates who would galvanise the support of the trusting who, in turn, would try to engage the cautious.

The Pharaoh finished by saying it was time to reap the benefits of the hard work of stage one – research, stage two – strategy and stage three – engagement, and turn that into productivity on the construction of the pyramid.

Before he left the meeting the Pharaoh asked the Sage what he would have to do next.

"That's easy. Make sure your officials fully understand every page of the map. Ensure also that they hold regular sessions with their people to re-affirm the contents. Support the Cultural Architects. Remember they are your great advocates and influencers of others. And last of all, remember to keep giving your people a good listening to."

"When will I meet up with you again?" asked the Pharaoh.

"I don't know," was the reply. "You have a lot to do. You will know when the time is right. What I do know is that the power of engagement is about to put your pyramid back on schedule."

Over the next few years the pyramid construction took on a life of its own. The people were truly engaged and the productivity reached a level never previously achieved.

The Cultural Architects played their part in supporting and communicating the Pharaoh's vision and, within two years, the pyramid had caught up to the schedule. Within five years it had gone far ahead. The hearts and minds of the people were very much on the journey. It was once again a great time to be an Egyptian and an even greater time to be a Pharaoh.

Lessons from the Journey

🦅 The Engagement stage focuses on obtaining 'buy in' and commitment from others to signing up and playing a personal part on the journey

🦅 It also describes the leadership approach to handling the three different groups of individuals in the workplace

🦅 Conscription does not guarantee commitment from others on the journey

🦅 The role of the leader is not to create more followers but to create more leaders – we call them Cultural Architects

🦅 Cultural Architects are advocates of the vision, the map and are proud to be associated with the journey

🦅 Carrying out a survey is a good way of measuring the effectiveness of the map and individual reaction to the journey

🦅 Remember each individual's perception is his reality. Acknowledge this, respect it and listen to him

🦅 An engaged workforce will create a productive workplace

🦅 Connection to the purpose of the journey and a feeling that individuals can contribute and make a difference are powerful engagement factors

🦅 The link between the workplace experience and the benefits to each individual also impacts on engagement levels

🦅 Trust and belief in the leaders are vital. Their performance and capability have the greatest impact on engagement levels

🦅 The journey map is the most important engagement tool in the leader's toolbox. It represents the leader's reputation and will help retain talent throughout the journey

🦅 Navigating the journey will require the leadership support of Cultural Architects

Stage Three: Engagement

*"The role of the leader is not to generate
more followers but to create more leaders"*

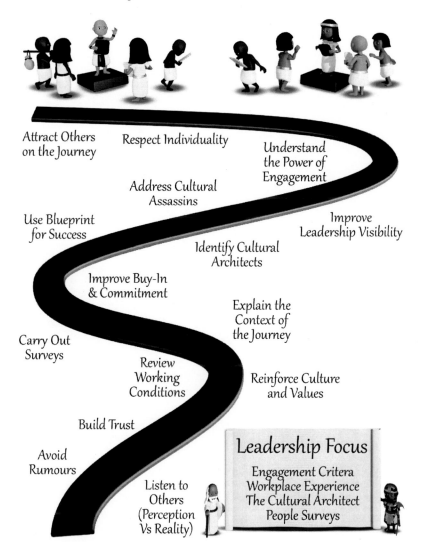

Attract Others
on the Journey

Respect Individuality

Understand
the Power of
Engagement

Address Cultural
Assassins

Use Blueprint
for Success

Improve
Leadership Visibility

Identify Cultural
Architects

Improve Buy-In
& Commitment

Explain the
Context of
the Journey

Carry Out
Surveys

Review
Working
Conditions

Reinforce Culture
and Values

Build Trust

Avoid
Rumours

Listen to
Others
(Perception
Vs Reality)

Leadership Focus

Engagement Critera
Workplace Experience
The Cultural Architect
People Surveys

Creating the Climate

"You shall rise with Orion in the western sky and set sail"

The Pharaoh was now ten years into the journey and the pyramid was more than half way to completion. The architect and his team had reported that, at the current work rate across all areas of the construction, the pyramid would be completed in seventeen years, three ahead of schedule.

The Pharaoh was delighted with the news. He was rightly proud of his team, and proud of the contribution of his people.

As construction picked up pace and met the planned schedules, the Pharaoh had less and less contact with Prem. When the pyramid-building project went ahead of schedule the Pharaoh decided there was no need to involve him further. Now it was just a matter of continuing the journey.

Smendes believed that he had personally devoted enough energy to the project and felt it was time to broaden his horizons and learn more about the world in which he lived. It was time, he thought, to experience life outside the kingdom. His mother would often tell him, before she departed for the New World, that he should see as much of the Old World as possible.

He announced that he would be taking a year out of the country.

He asked his team to contact him if they had any problems they couldn't handle. He assured them that they had his full confidence in managing the kingdom and continuing the pyramid-building journey.

A year later, he returned laden with riches, and full of experience and hope. He had learned a lot about other countries, their cultures, their expertise and their plans. He intended to use the knowledge and experience gained to make Egypt an even more prosperous and advanced nation than it was at that moment.

On his return journey, his thoughts were preoccupied with the progress of the pyramid. It was ten months since he had heard anything from his team. He assumed that all was well in the kingdom and that the pyramid was continuing to progress towards its completion.

However, as he got nearer to the capital, he could see that all was not well. He realised that the pyramid hadn't increased significantly in height. He also noticed that, although the people were obviously busy, the atmosphere was different.

He called a meeting of his officials and advisers to shed some light on the lack of progress. His team had not looked forward to his arrival back from his trip. They knew that progress had not been good, but they didn't know why. They were doing what they had always done and were confused about the situation. It was as if they had reached a plateau on their journey.

The Pharaoh discussed the events over the twelve-month period at great length. Everything seemed to be in place, but the Architect told the Pharaoh that if corrective action wasn't taken, the pyramid would never meet its twenty-year completion date. It was clearly time to pay Prem a visit, the Pharaoh thought. He would have the answer.

The Sage was delighted to meet the Pharaoh again. He had heard about the integration of the map into the kingdom and the success the Pharaoh had enjoyed in getting the pyramid construction ahead of schedule. He wasn't, however, surprised to hear about the plateau the Pharaoh was now experiencing.

He listened knowingly, as the Pharaoh listed the reasons why he thought the project had stalled.

First, he blamed himself for having gone away on his trip. His lack of visibility had resulted in a lack of focus on the construction project. Perhaps he had to be constantly on site, maintaining productivity and communicating with the workforce. It could also be that his team was not as good as he imagined they were. Finally, he questioned the journey map; perhaps it wasn't as fine a piece of work as he had thought.

"I assumed," said the Pharaoh, "that the journey map would solve all our problems; we had put enough work into it as a team. There was nothing more that I could have done personally to support the journey. To say that I am disappointed with where we are today is an understatement!"

Prem explained to the Pharaoh that one of the marks of a great leader is his or her ability to leave others to get on with the journey.

"Successful Pharaohs in the past," he explained, "including your mother, went on to carry out other important duties, and yet completed their pyramids on time. You were right to travel abroad. The knowledge and experience that you have gained will stand you in good stead for many years to come."

"Don't blame the map either," continued Prem. "A good manuscript doesn't become a bad manuscript overnight. There are other reasons why your progress has reached a plateau and it's time for us to discuss this as stage four of the journey – what I call motivation."

Prem explained that it was time to carry out another survey, although this would be a survey with a difference; it would involve only the two of them.

They spent a week visiting selected villages and cities around the capital to find out where the problems lay. They both travelled in disguise and, to the casual observer, looked like ordinary Egyptians going about their day-to-day business. No-one knew that they were in the presence of the ruler of the kingdom.

Both men merged into the village life, and listened to the farmers and craftsmen, ordinary men and women and even to the children. They uncovered a staggering picture of what life was like on the Pharaoh's pyramid journey. When they finally arrived back at the Royal Palace, they spent time putting together a detailed summary of life in the kingdom.

The summary included the following points:

•   The map had successfully played its part in announcing the Pharaoh's journey to the people of Egypt

•   Everyone in the kingdom still had a copy but very few people made reference to it

- Officials, managers and advisers in the kingdom had stopped using it or referring to it between themselves and with their teams

- New people joining the journey were given a copy and were expected to understand it. Very rarely was it explained to them in detail

- Although the people knew what the Pharaoh's vision was, they lacked focus on the journey

- The improvements that the Pharaoh had made, as a result of the previous survey with the people, had been forgotten by the majority of the population. New problems were occurring on a daily basis and were not addressed by managers and advisers

- The people were tired. They were promised ten days' work and one day of rest, but this very rarely happened

- Success on the journey was no longer celebrated as it was in the early days. It was now taken for granted by managers. They no longer saw the need to celebrate with their people

- On the sites, tools were not sharpened and returned quickly enough, sledges would often break and accidents were now happening on a daily basis

- Wives and partners were unhappy because their husbands and partners were unhappy

- There wasn't as much fun on the journey as there had been

- The journey had become too serious. Destination became the priority once again. Many of the old bad habits had resurfaced

- Sickness was up, particularly on a Monday. Hangovers from Sunday evenings became part of the new construction culture

- The Egyptian people believed that the journey would be completed, but the sense of urgency and passion had waned

- There were great inconsistencies regarding overall morale. People in the quarry felt undervalued and unrecognised for their efforts. The transport team felt ignored, while the people on the pyramid site appeared to get more rewards than others. The support people in the kingdom felt they were being taken for granted. A culture of arrogance and self-importance had crept into some of the teams. Some groups started to resent others

- The people very rarely knew how the journey was progressing. The public events that they had enjoyed before had stopped. The reasons given were that the Pharaoh was too busy looking at new opportunities for the kingdom.

When they had finished, the Pharaoh asked the Sage how to make sense of the findings. The people were clearly unhappy again.

Prem replied, "It's time to consider stage four of the formula. But you are tired after our travels. Come back tomorrow and we will study the importance of motivation."

After a good night's sleep, the Pharaoh was rested, but not relaxed. He summoned Prem immediately, hoping that he would be able to calm his mood.

When Prem arrived, the pair resumed their conversation from the night before. Pointing to the survey results that lay on the table in front of them, Prem started to explain that, contrary to their findings, the people had a lot to be happy about. They had a sense of purpose in their lives – the pyramid-building journey. The country was in good shape; food and water was in plentiful supply; their children were better educated than they had ever been and people were more informed within their communities.

"But look at the feedback we obtained on our visits. It's terrible!" exclaimed the Pharaoh.

"It's not terrible at all," Prem replied, "it's indicative of a group of people who have a higher expectation of themselves, their neighbours, their co-workers, their Pharaoh and their kingdom. They have learnt more and experienced more. As a result, the things that challenged and motivated them at the start of the journey no longer do so. They have moved on as individuals."

He explained to the Pharaoh that he had reached a critical stage in the journey. The foundations had been laid, the plans had been announced, the people had been engaged and the culmination was that progress so far had been spectacular. This was down to the motivation levels of the people. But those motivation levels had reached a plateau.

Prem described motivation as 'an internal driving force within an individual'. Every person in the kingdom had a driving force, a will to act in some way. High productivity on the pyramid construction resulted from a high driving force from each person, and low productivity from the opposite. But, Prem continued, the Pharaoh could not himself motivate people. All he could do was create the right climate where an individual's internal driving force could excel. He had successfully created such a climate when he involved the people in the contents of the map. Now he needed to set new standards.

The Sage smiled reassuringly. "The time to motivate your people is when they are already motivated."

Stage four was about creating a climate of performance, where the people would continue to be so motivated that their contribution would far exceed anything that had gone before. In order to create a climate of performance, he first had to remove any barriers affecting the internal driving force of his people.

"To help you and your team decide how motivated your people are, I have produced this list for you, which highlights the most important motivation factors that affect performance. Use this checklist to monitor the 'motivation' level within your teams. Most of the reasons why you are currently in the plateau are on this list. Most of our findings from our secret visits are also on this list. When you have the information take corrective action. This will make a difference to morale in your kingdom."

PEOPLE MOTIVATION FACTORS

- Understanding of the Vision
- Involvement level on the journey
- Opportunity to issue feedback
- Performance of the leaders
- Progress on the journey
- Level of on-the-job support
- Involvement in decision making
- Sense of belonging
- Making a difference
- Support from other colleagues
- Impact of other colleagues' work
- Training and development received
- Being part of something special
- Level of fun on the journey
- Strength of the communication grapevine
- Reward and recognition received
- Public events and social gatherings
- Perception of the Pharaoh
- The setting of realistic goals
- Meaning attached to the work
- Size of the opportunity or challenge
- Respect received in the workplace
- Sense of accomplishment
- Quality of the work environment
- Opportunities for advancement
- Relevance of personal contribution

Prem then explained that a fundamental part of creating a climate of performance was ensuring that four key principles were put in place. These were:

- Principle of Achievement

- Principle of Recognition

- Principle of Participation

- Principle of Growth

He explained that, used collectively or individually, they were key to meeting the higher expectations of his people on the pyramid-building journey. The longer his people were on the journey, the more important these principles would be.

He then explained each principle.

The Principle of Achievement would mean his people would require new goals, targets and journey markers to be set. They would quickly become bored of hitting the same target; the journey would not be challenging enough for them. As a result, they would look elsewhere to satisfy their hunger for new challenges in the future.

With regard to the Principle of Recognition, his people would demand new and innovative forms of reward for their efforts on the journey. They would no longer be inspired to break new boundaries on behalf of the Pharaoh, if they continued to receive the same 'thank you' response from him, or the same jar of wine as recognition of their efforts. The key to meeting their recognition requirements was to involve others: friends, families, work colleagues, and officials. The more public the recognition, the better.

In relation to the Principle of Participation, Prem reminded the Pharaoh of the impact the people survey and the map 'cascade' sessions had on the journey's early success. Like the previous two principles, new and more innovative methods would be required to appeal to the people's participation needs. They would need to be even more involved if they were to support him on the next leg of the journey.

Finally, he talked about the Principle of Growth. This was the principle most often neglected in stage four of the journey. As people learnt more about the Pharaoh, the journey and the kingdom, they would develop a thirst to grow and learn even more. If this need was not satisfied at a personal and work-based level, many of the people would feel unfulfilled. Eventually, this would be reflected in their productivity on the journey.

The Pharaoh listened attentively to the points made and could relate to the four principles, based on his own experience. "I remember, some of the best times I had as a child were when I was set a target and I achieved it, receiving public praise from my family. Often, it was when I was involved in the creation of something or when I learnt a new skill for the first time."

"The four principles that you speak of – Achievement, Recognition, Participation and Growth – combined to make me excel. I just never knew that the principles existed."

Prem then asked him to refer to the 'critical success factors' section of the journey map they had produced in stage three. He then explained to the Pharaoh that one of the biggest challenges he faced was to get everyone in the kingdom to contribute on a personal level to the contents of the map. The Pharaoh agreed. He was often told by sections of his people that the critical success factors applied to advisers and managers only.

Prem asked the Pharaoh to choose any one of the critical success factors for the purpose of the discussion. The Pharaoh chose the tools, equipment and resources factor, 'to provide the necessary tools, equipment and resources throughout the pyramid construction'.

"Who is responsible for the achievement of this objective?"

"That's easy" replied the Pharaoh, "It's the Operations Director."

"Who else has a part to play?"

"Probably, the Quarry Manager and one or two other people."

"Is that all?" asked Prem. "There must be more."

And then realisation dawned. When the Pharaoh thought about it, he realised that there were thousands of people who contributed. There were the labourers in the forests who supplied the wood, the carpenters who shaped the tools, the craftsmen who supplied the stone flints and copper blades. And then there were the women who bound the tools together, the boys who cleaned them, the transport team who delivered them, the storage people who kept them safe and secure and finally the supervisors who distributed them. Thousands of people contribute to provide the necessary tools, equipment and resources throughout the construction.

The Pharaoh summarised this thought. "We are only as strong as the weakest stone in the pyramid. If any of these people fail to play their part, then the journey is affected. I now understand the part that each person can play."

For the next few hours they discussed each critical success factor. Whether it was the supply of food and water, the security of the kingdom or the health and safety of the nation, the Pharaoh realised that, in every instance, many more people could play a part in supporting each factor.

"If you can get everyone in the kingdom to set personal targets and to list the behaviours and activity that they can bring to each 'Critical success factor', and then ask them to commit to supporting them on the journey, the vision – the end result – will be achieved a lot quicker," Prem said.

"Consider this," he continued, "if twenty thousand people each day are focused on their personal target and contribute five behaviours to the journey, one-hundred-thousand activities will happen which will bring you closer to your dream of the perfect pyramid. Now that is indeed impressive."

The Pharaoh agreed.

"Now you must sit down with your team, and discuss our survey findings. Then use the content to demonstrate your understanding of the four principles and produce a motivation plan for the kingdom. Producing this plan will enable you to motivate your people when they are already motivated."

Two weeks later, Prem once again found himself at the palace, this time being met by a far more enthusiastic Smendes. "My team and I have worked very hard since we last saw you," he explained. "We discussed motivation and have produced a plan linked to creating a climate of outstanding performance."

The Pharaoh handed Prem a document outlining their plan of action.

Under the 'Achievement' heading there were a series of points, including:

- New goals and targets would be set for the next leg of the journey

- High officials, advisers and managers would demonstrate to the people of Egypt how these would be achieved

- The people would be encouraged to monitor their own performance

A further set of points were included under the 'Recognition' heading, including:

- A reward and recognition scheme would be produced which would involve everyone in the Kingdom of Egypt

- The scheme would be linked to the four parts of the construction process (quarry, transport, pyramid site and support in the kingdom)

- Public celebrations and events would be organised to communicate the journey's progress, achievements and recognition of individuals and teams

The third heading was 'Participation':

- The people of Egypt would have more day-to-day involvement with the managers and advisers on the journey

- This would involve feedback sessions with the Pharaoh and his senior team

- The people would take responsibility for future surveys, reward recognition and communication events

Under the fourth section, 'Growth', the team had included the following:

- An education programme, including refresher forums, would be produced, explaining in detail the component parts of the Pharaoh's journey

- Personal behaviours and activity linked to the critical success factors would be included as part of the education process

- New innovation working groups would look at ways to improve efficiency across the four parts of the construction process

The Pharaoh then proceeded to present a sample of some of the motivation plans the team had produced. The plans were in their first draft but included activity linked to ensuring that people would improve their performance throughout the kingdom.

The motivation plans included more creative use of the journey map, the development of the people's working environment, public social events and gatherings, special competitions and awards, and lots of communication regarding the progress made on the journey. In each plan Achievement, Recognition, Participation and Growth were included.

Prem congratulated the Pharaoh on the work completed by his team.

"You have made impressive progress sir, and should be very pleased. You have successfully completed stage four of the journey. Now you must implement all that you have learnt."

The Pharaoh thanked him for his help and told him that he would be in touch.

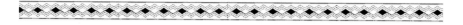

Lessons from the Journey

- The Motivation stage focuses on the creation and reinforcement of a performance climate in the workplace

- It also describes the leadership approach to identifying and understanding the barriers to high-performance working

- Motivation describes 'personal drive'. Leaders and managers will never be able to motivate their people. Individuals motivate themselves

- The leader's role is to understand the factors which contribute to the motivation level of individuals and provide the resources and support required to enable them to perform to their potential

- Leaders should carry out regular surveys to gauge the motivation levels of their people

- Communication (or lack of it) are powerful demotivators in the workplace and will dramatically affect performance

- Every aspect of the leader's day-to-day role should focus on the achievement, recognition, participation and growth principles

- Achievement is the number one motivation force in the workplace

- Performance measures for each area of the workplace should be aligned to the overall goals to be achieved on the journey

- Recognition is a powerful force. Make it public. Remember the greater the performance, the greater the celebration should be

- Participation is important too. Everyone want to be part of something special

- Linking behaviours and activity to each role in the workplace supports growth

- Navigating the journey will require a working environment conducive to the needs of a high-performing organisation

Stage Four: Motivation

"The role of the leader is to create a climate which will enable others to perform to their full potential"

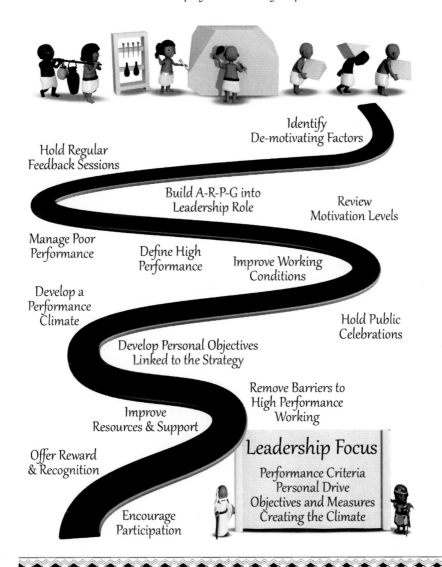

Identify
De-motivating Factors

Hold Regular
Feedback Sessions

Build A-R-P-G into
Leadership Role

Review
Motivation Levels

Manage Poor
Performance

Define High
Performance

Improve Working
Conditions

Develop a
Performance
Climate

Hold Public
Celebrations

Develop Personal Objectives
Linked to the Strategy

Remove Barriers to
High Performance
Working

Improve
Resources & Support

Offer Reward
& Recognition

Leadership Focus

Performance Criteria
Personal Drive
Objectives and Measures
Creating the Climate

Encourage
Participation

Protecting Good Work

"There grows no wheat where there is no grain"

The Pharaoh visited Prem a few months later. "Good morning your Royal Highness," said the Sage. "I didn't expect to see you for some time."

"I have a great deal to do," replied the Pharaoh, "but I wasn't going to make the same mistake twice. I know that there are six stages to the formula. To date, you've only told me about four of them. Although we have started our work on the next stage, I thought you would discuss stages five and six with me."

"Very well sir," said Prem. "I will do half of what you ask. I'll discuss stage five of the journey with you today – development. This stage follows on quickly from stage four and in some respects has a degree of overlap, particularly with regards to growth."

The Sage went on to explain that, although performance levels would again be strong as a result of the new activities, the Pharaoh had to be careful because accidents and unforeseen circumstances would require an additional impetus to take the journey on to its completion. These accidents and unforeseen circumstances related directly to the success of the journey. He explained that one of a number of things could now happen.

1. The people would become more productive but some would find the work less challenging than before

2. As a result, they would look elsewhere for new challenges

3. They would be influenced by others to join up on a different journey

4. They would realise that they had grown as part of the journey and that they now had the potential for greater things

5. They might look to use their talent elsewhere

6. There would be a constant turnover of people throughout the journey. Some would leave and some would die

7. New people joining would not have the same emotional tie as others who have been on the journey from the beginning; therefore engagement could be more difficult to achieve with this group

8. If anything could go wrong, then it probably would

9. People would continue to have a higher expectation of their leaders

10. The closer to the end of the journey, the easier it would be for people to lose focus

He highlighted that the constantly changing personnel over the period of the pyramid's construction would create difficulties for the Pharaoh. Quality would be affected at a critical time on the journey because of the loss of knowledge and expertise throughout the kingdom. Many pyramids in the desert were left unfinished as a result of this.

Prem explained that stage five involved preparing for every eventuality, in effect, producing an even stronger structure of support. It was time to protect the good work of the past and look at how the pyramid-building process could be further improved.

"I don't believe we have anything to worry about," said Smendes. "Everything is in place. Our leaders have created the climate we need, everyone has a personal target to reach and we are on schedule to complete the construction."

"Let's go for a walk," replied Prem. "We need to observe the progress of the construction and the behaviours demonstrated by your people. This time let's not comment as we walk. We'll just observe what's going on and discuss our thoughts when we get back to the palace."

At first, Smendes found the observational exercise and the silence between each of them unbearable. But after a few hours he found the process enlightening. Words didn't need to be spoken to convey what was happening across the various sites – it was clear for all to see.

Some aspects of the pyramid construction were completed to a very high standard, whilst other elements remained unfinished. Teams were performing well on some sites, while other teams working a few yards away from them were struggling to cope. Many individuals demonstrated ability and confidence beyond their years. Others demonstrated naivety. There was a lack of consistency of quality, purpose and teamwork across the sites, and this worried Smendes.

When they arrived back at the palace the King could contain himself no longer.

"I just don't get it," he exploded. "Where have we gone wrong? Everyone is busy, but mistakes are still being made."

"Why are you so hard on yourself?" asked Prem. "The perfect pyramid takes time. Your people are working hard, but this is where the important lessons of stage five come in to play."

"The development stage on the journey is much more than protecting your work: it's also about protecting your people – not from others – but from themselves."

"What do you mean?" asked the Pharaoh.

It's human nature for some people to become complacent when work is going well," replied Prem.

"But did you notice the selfish nature of some individuals and teams as they watched others struggle? What are they thinking about and why are they not supporting their colleagues? There was no work between teams. I also couldn't believe that we are using methods and tools that were appropriate ten years ago but clearly are not right for these times. Complacency has crept in alright and a lot of people are oblivious to it."

Prem tried to calm him down. "It's easy to get locked into focusing on your own area of work but, as you saw, if you wish to build a great workforce, then everyone will have to understand and support the needs of others. This involves a review of work practices and a greater focus on innovation and efficiency on the journey. Information and the use of it is important to your success."

Smendes was confused. "But surely individuals don't need to know everything about everything – that will only confuse them."

"Of course not," replied Prem, "but every member of your workforce needs to know certain things. They need to have a general overview of the project and the systems and processes used in the day-to-day construction process. They also need to understand the skills and competencies required to do their own jobs, and the challenges facing the people that they have daily contact with.

"Protecting the good work involves everyone in the kingdom," said the Sage. "Each person needs to understand the impact their performance and attitude has on others around them. They also need to identify the reasons for mistakes and inefficiency. They need to respect the cost of inefficiency and develop a passion for continuous improvement. More importantly, they have to maximise the use of information and experience, pass it on, share it and be comfortable sharing it."

Prem explained that unlocking the value of knowledge and sharing it with others was an important element of stage five of the journey, and vital to improving efficiency.

The Pharaoh agreed and reflected on the loss of data and experience over the years. How he wished he had taken the necessary steps to protect and safeguard it at the time.

But although Smendes appreciated Prem's words, he thought to himself it was easier said than done. Over the years, he had met many people who used information to court favour or demonstrate power. "How will we achieve this?" he asked.

"We will use a system called the wheel of learning," replied Prem.

Prem explained that the 'wheel of learning' was a development process linked to maximising operational efficiency. It enabled people to be creative and at the same time cope with change in the workplace.

The process encourages individuals to carry out four functions – to understand, to challenge, to improve and to change – linked to how they work and how others work. By carrying out each function, information is shared, excellence is achieved, innovation is encouraged and teamwork begins. The combination of all four areas of focus results in constant and continuous improvement and higher levels of performance.

"The role of the leaders is vitally important to learning," said Prem. "Learning is the legacy we should all leave to others. Learning by understanding, by challenging, by improving and by changing. The role of your leaders is to lead by listening, by observing and by encouraging others to learn by doing."

"Learning has to be led and inspired by leaders. It's a skill and an attitude that applies to everyone, regardless of status. It should be applied throughout life. Some people call it lifelong learning."

"Your people should remember that if they are not growing then the kingdom is not growing and this starts by understanding the important contribution that they and others play in the success of the journey."

The Pharaoh fully understood Prem's thinking, and was disappointed that the team hadn't thought of it before.

"The starting point of information sharing is defining what you mean by 'perfect,'" Prem continued. "In order to produce the perfect pyramid, you will need to explain what 'perfect' looks like to your people. You will have to present an overview of the pyramid-building model highlighting in simple language where everyone fits in to the construction process. As soon as they understand this, they can begin to help you improve efficiency."

Smendes looked puzzled.

"Secondly, you need to identify and produce a set of systems and processes which can be understood and supported by everyone on the journey. The scribes will be involved in their documentation. The manuscript will be discussed by the people, developed by the people and finally produced by the people."

Prem continued by telling Smendes that many of the people would be even more engaged in the journey at the thought of producing such a fine piece of work. The systems and processes manuscript would be a presentation of their pride in their work and the attention to detail required to succeed. It would also act as a reference guide should anyone be unsure of any aspect of the construction process.

"They would learn a great deal from carrying out the process, and it would satisfy their need for growth," said the Sage.

Although the Pharaoh acknowledged the thinking behind the advice, he didn't like the idea of producing a construction manual. What if it got into the wrong hands? He explained his concerns to Prem who, although he respected the Pharaoh's uneasiness, felt that the benefits on the journey would far outweigh his concerns.

"You could always ensure that the copy is kept secure and safe. On your journey from the Old World to the New World, the manuscript would join you. The pyramid would be sealed and no person would ever be able to get their hands on it."

The Pharaoh agreed that he would discuss it with the architect and his team.

Prem continued, "The theme of perfection applies to skills and competencies in the workplace. An important part of the leaders' role is to encourage individuals to assess their role and to identify the knowledge, skills and behaviours required to deliver perfection. It will be different for each individual. Perfection for the stonemasons will be different to the carpenters, and so on.

"When people are aware of what 'perfect' looks like they can strive to achieve it by delivering higher levels of personal performance. Growth is a powerful motivation for many people."

The Pharaoh agreed. He had established the principles for growth in his outstanding performance document in stage four. He now needed to be mindful of this link and continue to appreciate its importance.

Prem went on to discuss teamworking. He reminded the Pharaoh of the reaction to the vision he and his team had produced several years earlier. As a single piece of work it had truly moved mountains. People were, for the first time, aware of what the journey entailed throughout its passage.

He went on to suggest that it was time to transfer the lessons learned from the Pharaoh's vision into the production of new visions, one for each operational area of the construction process. By developing these visions at a more personal level, the people would be able to connect more closely with the Pharaoh's vision.

Smendes smiled, "Every team needs a team vision don't they? It makes it easier for individuals to understand their contribution, where they fit in and how to support the group. The team vision can then be shared with other teams. When each team understands each other's vision they are better placed to be able to help them overcome their challenges and issues on a daily basis."

"Simple but effective," replied Prem. "A pyramid vision underpinned by site visions supported by team vision."

"I now understand the secret to leading the kingdom. It's all about vision, its understanding and how it's used to inspire millions of people."

Prem told the Pharaoh that he had finished his education relating to stage five and that his journey would soon be completed.

"This is excellent news. So what about stage six?" asked the Pharaoh. "Are you not going to explain it to me now?"

"No" replied Prem, "when the time is right I would prefer you to explain it to me. You will soon know what it is, and when it has been completed."

"Stage six is when the pyramid is complete!" declared the Pharaoh.

"You decide," replied Prem.

Smendes travelled back to the palace and held a debrief meeting with his high officials.

Knowledge sharing and the use of experience would become a cultural norm throughout the kingdom. The Chief Architect offered to produce hundreds of small scale models of the pyramid and the sites to help explain the construction process to the people, particularly in the village regions. The leaders were tasked with holding 'perfect sessions' with their teams to identify the skills and competencies required for each role. And a Head of Operational Efficiency was appointed to review and develop teams and their teamworking capability across the country.

Over dinner the King reflected on the day's events and the wheel of learning. He decided that stone wheels would be produced and placed throughout the kingdom explaining the system with Egyptian images depicting understanding, challenging, improving and changing. Above each wheel was the slogan, 'Learn by doing, live by learning'.

For the first time in a long time he was confident that the journey was near to completion. The stress had at times made it difficult for him to sleep but not on this night. He felt a strange sense of calmness. As soon as his head hit the pillow he dreamt of his ultimate achievement.

The perfect pyramid was within his grasp.

Lessons from the Journey

- The Development stage focuses on the protection of the work that has gone before and the commitment to setting new and higher standards in the future

- It also describes the leadership approach to improving operational efficiency in the workplace through learning

- Unlocking the power of information and experience and sharing it with others is vital to achieving success on the journey

- The view of the journey is different from person to person. Try to get everyone to view the journey through the Pharaoh's eyes

- The leader's role is to inspire everyone on the journey to commit to the wheel of learning

- The wheel of learning enables people to understand, challenge, improve and change how they and others work

- Systems and processes improve through innovation and people improve through learning. The combination of both results in change for the better

- Skills and competencies will always change in line with the demands of each person's role and its purpose. If people aren't growing the kingdom isn't growing

- Individual focus on improving skills and competencies linked to each role will result in the perfect pyramid

- Every individual in some way directly impacts on the performance and outcomes of others. Effective team working and inter-team working are vital to operational efficiency

- A commitment to learning across the workforce avoids complacency creeping in

- Navigating the journey will require a commitment to innovation, change and 'new ways of working'

Stage Five: Development

"The role of the leader is to protect the systems, processes and people important to creating a sustainable long standing pyramid"

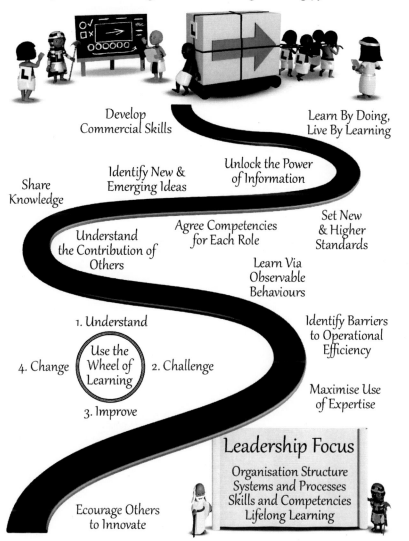

Develop Commercial Skills

Learn By Doing, Live By Learning

Identify New & Emerging Ideas

Unlock the Power of Information

Share Knowledge

Set New & Higher Standards

Understand the Contribution of Others

Agree Competencies for Each Role

Learn Via Observable Behaviours

1. Understand

Use the Wheel of Learning

4. Change

2. Challenge

Identify Barriers to Operational Efficiency

3. Improve

Maximise Use of Expertise

Leadership Focus

Organisation Structure
Systems and Processes
Skills and Competencies
Lifelong Learning

Ecourage Others to Innovate

The Ultimate Goal

*"Ride alone in the chariot drawn by inspiration and you
will be followed by eager fanbearers"*

The performance of the workforce reached new levels and the construction of
the pyramid was on schedule. The King relaxed more and as a result of the
progress being made, began to enjoy the journey and the prospect of one day
reaching the New World.

After a particularly busy day involving the design of new robes planned for
the celebration of the expected pyramid completion, Smendes enjoyed the best
night's sleep in years. When he woke up he found his room strangely quiet.
There wasn't the normal buzz of servants preparing for the day ahead.

He got out of bed and made his way to the corner of the room. As he opened the
shuttered window to greet the new day, instead of the beautiful landscape image
of Egypt and his kingdom he was met with a picture of devastation and disaster.

"What the.......servant, servant," he shouted. After what seemed like an eternity
his loyal servant arrived.

"What has happened?" shouted Smendes.

The servant proceeded to inform the King that in the middle of the night, the
country had been hit with one of the biggest storms in its history. The banks of
the Nile had burst, flooding most of the immediate area. Thunder had frightened
the people and lightning had struck the pyramid, causing devastation to the
top level including the area around the apex. An earthquake had also occurred,
damaging the roads and infrastructure en route to the pyramid.

"Why didn't you wake me up?" cried Smendes.

"We didn't like to, you looked so peaceful and you did say to only wake you in
the event of an emergency."

"Well what was last night then if not an emergency?"

"A challenge," whispered the confused servant.

"Summon the advisers, get the Royal Barge and chariot ready. We need to address the situation with immediate effect."

"You are too late," said the servant.

"What do you mean, I'm too late?" shouted the King. Smendes feared the worst for his kingdom and his perfect pyramid. It was only when he conducted a tour of the construction site that he understood the true meaning of the servant's words.

Some weeks later, the Pharaoh arrived at Prem's home to announce that he was ready to talk to him about stage six of the journey.

"I'm going to take you on a tour of the kingdom. I want you to see how we are doing for yourself."

Prem was intrigued by the Pharaoh's proposal. As they began the tour, the Pharaoh explained to Prem that he was going to witness the culmination of the previous five stages: research, strategy, engagement, motivation and development, plus the secrets of stage six of the formula.

They arrived at the quarry first. There was a real sense of activity and excitement. The Sage was impressed by the attention to detail in such a physically demanding part of the construction. He noticed that the foremen had introduced competitions and, at set times in the operation, the work would stop and public awards would be made. Each team had a clear identity of its own and a real sense of purpose.

"Isn't it impressive?" said the Pharaoh, "A real world demonstration of confidence, certainty of purpose and synergy."

Prem could only agree.

They next visited the transport operation, where the stones were moved out of the quarry. Prem noticed that everyone was singing as they pulled the sledges.

The operation was impressive, with everyone working in tandem to ensure that no time was wasted between the quarry and the pyramid site.

"We've never moved as much stone per day as we do today. Look at the sledge operation. See how two men pour water on the bottom of the sledge. This lubricates it, enabling the stone to be carried quicker. This idea came from the people. We explain our problems to them now, and every time they come up with the solutions."

"What is that man doing?" asked Prem.

"He's helping us produce our manuscript, which details the systems, processes and approach we should take to ensure that we maintain maximum efficiency on the journey. We decided it was a good idea. We have an official who champions it and hundreds of men and women who support the development of the manuscript. They are everywhere on the journey," replied the Pharaoh.

They travelled up the Nile to visit the pyramid site. In one of the villages they could see women baking cakes, with baskets of figs and others fruits already out on display.

"This village has just won a competition for the best improvement in production over the past three months. Tonight they will be holding their own celebration banquet. You can see how excited they are – and why not? They deserve it," said the Pharaoh.

When they arrived at the quayside Prem was amazed at the sheer scale of the pyramid site. He noticed that many officials had already built tombs alongside the Causeway so they could be with the King when he died.

The huge tomb by now looked like a pyramid. The Pharaoh led the way up onto the structure. He wanted to show Prem the workmanship of his people.

"Look at this," he said. "One after another, perfect blocks, all cut and aligned with great precision. There isn't a single space between each block. Have you noticed that we never use mortar to hold the blocks together?"

Prem now knew what the Pharaoh had meant when he said he wanted to create the perfect pyramid.

The Pharaoh went on to explain that they had developed elite teams that they could use to identify what was required to truly excel on the construction. The lessons they had learned were now being passed on to others. Productivity had increased, but so had quality.

Throughout the pyramid site they witnessed leadership, teamwork, quality, innovation and efficiency. The Sage could see how proud the Pharaoh was of his people. He couldn't stop talking about their achievements.

At the palace, Prem was introduced to the Director of Development, who was tasked with all growth issues on the journey. She had produced education, development and leadership programmes. Everyone in the kingdom had a growth programme. She had linked each programme to the Pharaoh's 'Journey Map' and had ensured that action planning, linked to each person's contribution on the journey, was at the core of the programme.

Cultural Architects received specialist support. Regular public forums and meetings were held and the Director of Development was also responsible for the management of the people survey. Lastly, a career planning programme had been developed to ensure that when people were too ill or too old to continue on the journey, new recruits would take over.

Unbeknown to Prem, the Pharaoh had organised a special dinner in honour of the Sage's contribution on the journey. He had invited members of his team and other high officials to the event.

As they sat and enjoyed the meal, Prem thanked the Pharaoh for the day. "It was truly impressive to witness the work," he said.

The Pharaoh told Prem that he could now see more clearly the journey he was on. He also believed that he knew the final component part of his formula; the secret stage six of the journey. Prem had waited all day and for the previous thirteen years for this moment.

"You are eager to tell me something, sir," he said with a smile.

"Stage six of the formula is ownership," replied the Pharaoh.

"How did you work it out?" asked Prem.

"Well we had a bit of a flood, or as my servant called it – a challenge. Our gods decided to examine our capability. I won't bore you with the details but our people have been put to the ultimate test involving a mixture of lightning, high floods and the moving of earth. Three forces of nature designed to see if we could finish the journey."

"My goodness, were you not in a panic?"

Smendes then went on to explain to Prem the meaning of ownership.

"Well of course, I was in a panic. I was also annoyed that I wasn't woken up to lead the team to resolve the disaster. My servant kept on telling me that I was too late and I thought he meant I was too late to do anything. When I arrived at the various sites, I was too late to start leading the clear up and restoration. The work had already started and the people had everything in hand."

The King proceeded to explain to Prem the meaning of ownership and how it played a part in clearing up the mess from the natural disasters and keeping the construction project on track and on time.

The leaders had inspired and empowered their people to do 'what was appropriate and necessary'. The workforce demonstrated ingenuity, teamwork and focus. They used the flooded landscape to take boats full of new stones and pulleys right up to the side of the pyramid to carry out the repair work on the apex. They used the power of water to carry out duties in minutes that would previously have taken months to achieve. When the work was completed, they drained the Nile water by redirecting it using the enormous cracks in the ground caused by the earthquake.

"How did the teams learn how to do that?" asked Prem.

"Well they didn't; how could you learn such a task?" replied Smendes.

"What was impressive was that each and every individual took personal responsibility for their part in the emergency operation. They knew how to behave, what to do, what decisions to make, and never once did they look to question the contribution of others. They didn't even blame our gods for what had happened.

"They revisited the content in our journey map and used it to adjust their actions and behaviours to deal effectively with the disaster and devastation they were faced with. The Cultural Architects supported the leaders by communicating to others worried about the events unfolding throughout the kingdom. They were able to build trust with our people and, as a result, a plentiful supply of food, water and tools were made available for those people working on the pyramid. Everyone played their part.

"I learnt that ownership is stage six of the journey and the ultimate goal of any leader. It is about empowering others to give their best. It is about building self-confidence. Ownership cannot be forced on the people. Individuals must want to take responsibility and my people demonstrated this in spades and bucket loads. I am so proud of them.

"Do you know something Prem, I could leave the kingdom, search out new experiences, perhaps have a holiday or visit other Kings, and because of ownership I would be confident that on my return Egypt would be in great shape. That's how confident I am about my people."

Prem was beaming. "Congratulations your Royal Highness. Ownership is indeed the final stage of the journey and as you have demonstrated, it is the sign that your people are prepared for every eventuality they are likely to face in the future.

"It's a moment on the journey when they instinctively know that their performance will play a significant part in the success and realisation of the vision. They also trust each other and know they can rely on each colleague to support them – whatever happens.

"Ownership is also focused on the execution of the plan produced at the beginning of the journey, and to many Pharaohs it's the most important element of the journey."

The Pharaoh agreed.

"It's all very well producing a vision of what the perfect pyramid could look like, but the biggest challenge facing all leaders is delivering it, and with everyone with you. To quote a Pharaoh from the past, 'A vision without action will not take you to the New World.'"

The Ultimate Goal

Lessons from the Journey

- The Ownership stage focuses on maximising the performance potential of every individual in the workplace

- It also describes the leadership approach to developing 'personal accountability'

- Leaders will never achieve ownership if individuals are not committed to the journey

- The ability to handle last-minute problems, surprising challenges and disasters are measures of ownership effectiveness

- Ownership is about being aware of the environment in which people operate and taking the appropriate action to maximise their personal performance

- Understanding the link between personal behaviour and personal outcomes is important to achieving ownership amongst the workforce

- Ownership evolves as a result of a clear understanding of each individual's role and responsibility on the journey

- Being part of something special makes it easier for individuals to take responsibility for their contribution

- Leaders are responsible for building up the confidence of their workforce

- The higher the sense of pride on the journey, the greater the sense of ownership and self-confidence that will be achieved

- Trust in leaders, colleagues and other teams is important to achieving ownership

- Ownership contributes to the effective execution of the strategy and enables leaders to achieve success on the journey and reach the end destination

- Navigating the journey will require the collective focus of everyone

Stage Six: Ownership

"The role of the leader is to build a confident, high performing workforce resulting in the successful execution of the strategy"

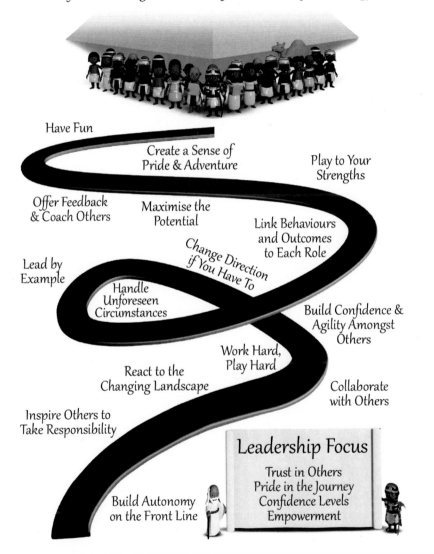

Have Fun

Create a Sense of
Pride & Adventure

Play to Your
Strengths

Offer Feedback
& Coach Others

Maximise the
Potential

Link Behaviours
and Outcomes
to Each Role

Change Direction
if You Have To

Lead by
Example

Handle
Unforeseen
Circumstances

Build Confidence &
Agility Amongst
Others

Work Hard,
Play Hard

React to the
Changing Landscape

Collaborate
with Others

Inspire Others to
Take Responsibility

Leadership Focus

Trust in Others
Pride in the Journey
Confidence Levels
Empowerment

Build Autonomy
on the Front Line

Reflection from a Pharaoh

The King and the Sage celebrated stage six and drank long into the night.

"And what of you personally. What have you learnt from the journey?" asked Prem.

The Pharaoh thought for a few moments and answered. "I've learnt that building the pyramid involved three different journeys running alongside each other, almost together."

"The first journey involves the actual construction process," he continued. "This involved the experts and the people I had around me. They knew what to do and there was no need for me to interfere with their job function."

"The second journey involved the use of the formula, the six stages. The more we learnt, the more we understood, and the more we understood the more we believed in what was possible. The use of the formula was as important as the day-to-day construction work."

"Using the formula also taught me about the power of engagement and that, more than anything, creating a sense of purpose and belonging was a key element in our success. The journey also had to be a pleasure. We spend too much time at work for it not to be enjoyable."

Prem smiled to himself, thinking how far the Pharaoh had come from his original proclamations and orders.

"And I learnt that the formula involved understanding the link between behaviour and results. Because of this and the work in the six stages, we are about to complete the perfect pyramid well ahead of schedule."

"The third journey was a different one, but in many ways as important a journey to take. I call it the 'journey of life' because the six stages of the formula apply to each and every one of us."

The Pharaoh continued.

"Everyone in the kingdom, at sometime in their life, wants to build a pyramid. By that I mean they have a dream or a vision that they want to realise in the future. This will involve a journey that they will have to embark on. They therefore will have to do some research and identify the size of the opportunity.

"If they want to be successful, they will then have to use this information and produce a journey map. After that, they need to surround themselves with people who they trust and who can engage in the journey with them. They will then have to remain motivated, ensuring their internal driving force is high. They will also have to remove any factors that could affect their progress on the journey.

"Continuing to personally grow, by developing new skills and knowledge, will be necessary to complete the journey successfully. Finally, they will need to take responsibility for the achievement of their vision by identifying the behaviours needed to succeed and applying them to ensure they are successful.

"The six stages of the formula apply as much to a person's life journey as they strive to build their own pyramid as they do to the ruler of Egypt."

Prem continued to listen intently.

"Let me add this," said the Pharaoh. "At the beginning, I thought that my main concern was just about the Old World and my passage to the New World. That is, of course, still important, but so is the Real World, which is why we are here today. I understand now why you often say that you have helped many people build many pyramids."

Prem nodded in agreement before asking, "What challenges do you think you now face?"

"Only one," replied the Pharaoh. "To pass on some of your teachings to my son, the next Pharaoh. I won't tell him everything. I understand why my mother didn't tell me everything. Learning is often more interesting when you are living through the experience."

"Is there anything more you would like to ask me?" queried Prem.

"Two things. You asked me on the day of my mother's funeral why I thought so many people attended. At the time I was surprised by the question. Tell me now, why did so many people honour her?"

"The ultimate compliment that your people can pay you is to attend your funeral," replied Prem. "Unfortunately, you will never witness it for yourself. But if the final component of stage six, ownership, has been achieved your people will be proud to turn up to your funeral and say, 'I helped the Pharaoh realise his vision. I helped the Pharaoh on his onward journey'."

The Pharaoh listened. "You are right. I suppose that the vision doesn't belong to the Pharaoh, it belongs to everyone. That is also when you realise that ownership has been achieved."

The Sage agreed.

"I have one last question. Although you refer to it as the formula, I understand that the real world title for the six stages is the winning (formula)®. Why is it called the winning formula?" asked the Pharaoh.

Prem paused for a moment before replying. "If used properly, everyone in the kingdom wins. There are no losers on the journey. You won because you realised your dream, the officials and advisers won because they contributed and the people won because of their satisfaction with the completed work."

As the evening came to a close, the Pharaoh publicly thanked Prem for his efforts, and announced that he had some good news for everyone. The pyramid would be completed by the end of the year, six years ahead of schedule. Everyone in the room rejoiced and clapped their hands with approval. All were united in their delight.

The evening was drawing to a close and the Pharaoh started to wish the Sage farewell.

"We got off to a bad start, and for that I'm sorry," Smendes said. "We've worked well together since, though, and I have learned a great deal from you. I now understand why my mother held you in such high esteem. I would never have completed the journey without you."

"You are right to say that you have completed the journey," replied Prem. "You trusted in me and listened to all that I said. You have succeeded in each stage of the journey, and have the full support of the people of Egypt. And look at what you have achieved as a result." He paused. "It is time that I gave you something very precious. It is a letter from your mother. I was instructed to give this to you when I judged that your journey was complete. That time is now."

The Pharaoh's mouth opened wide in surprise. He held out his hand to take the sheets of paper from Prem, and gingerly unfolded them.

My dear son,

If you are reading this letter, then you will have completed your pyramid. Congratulations, I am proud of you and although I hope that I won't meet up with you for many years to come, I look forward to celebrating your achievement with you.

I know that the journey would have been challenging for you. All Pharaohs have experienced what you have been through, but I never doubted your ability and determination to complete your perfect pyramid on time.

Working with any outsider can be difficult for a leader, but I hope you realise that Prem's role was to share his framework with you in a way which would offer you structure, confidence and direction.

The formula is an empowering process – rare in our world – which enables leaders to put their own personality and mark on their journey. At the same time, they are able to make decisions and take actions that they believe are right.

I'm sure you will agree that the formula has helped you and others around you to respond, adapt and change to the many circumstances and obstacles which have tested you over the years. I trust you did not meet any natural disasters along the way – they rarely occur.

Your pyramid is a reflection of the values which you yourself hold dear – passion, excellence and innovation.

You demonstrated these as a child and as a young man. I know you would have focused on these as Egypt's ruler. The pyramid is also a testament to your people, because without them the construction would not have been completed to your and everyone's satisfaction.

You will know by now the meaning behind the words "great is a great one whose great ones are great".

Your people are now emotionally connected to the pyramid – they will forever remember the journey – and they will want to continue to play an important part in protecting it in their lifetime. This will be a new journey for you and them.

So what must you do now?

There is always much to do throughout the country – so continue to look after your people. Focus on creating a dynamic and energising workplace where challenge is an important part of work. More importantly, ensure that there is real meaning to their work. Without it, complacency will set in and your good work will be undone.

It is also your responsibility as the ruler of Egypt to leave your mark on the environment. Remember to leave the old world in a better place than when you arrived. It is our world and we should look after it. Encourage others to do the same.

Finally, everyone wishes to be part of something special – a journey, a kingdom, perhaps a business or organisation. With that in mind, encourage the use of the formula. The six areas should always be at the heart of everything that people do. All journeys start in the heart with a desire and feeling to realise an authentic vision. Inspire others to develop their own visions and support them in the realisation of their dreams.

Best wishes on your next journey, wherever it may take you.

Your loving mother

Personal Reflection Exercise

Personal Reflection
Exercise

1. What aspects of the Pharaoh's journey can you most relate to?

2. How would you best describe your organisation's current performance?

3. What do you believe are the main challenges facing your organisation?

4. What is your understanding of your organisation's vision for the future?

5. What will you do differently to support your organisation on its journey?

Your Organisation's Journey

Personal notes and action planning checklist

Research - The size of the opportunity

- ☐
- ☐
- ☐

Strategy - The production of the route map

- ☐
- ☐
- ☐

Engagement - The buy-in and commitment to the growth plan

- ☐
- ☐
- ☐

Motivation - The creation of the performance climate

- ☐
- ☐
- ☐

Development - The protection of systems, processes and people

- ☐
- ☐
- ☐

Ownership -The maximisation of people potential

- ☐
- ☐
- ☐

Building your own Pyramid

The winning (formula)® Framework

I hope you have enjoyed reading *Building the Pyramid*. The storyline concept is designed to give you an understanding of the winning (formula)® – our people-based approach to delivering growth and success.

Your role as a leader is to inspire, guide and influence others in a way in which they will help you maximise the potential of your organisation. Transferring the lessons learned from the Pharaoh's journey to the real world of work and how they apply to your organisation will help you achieve this.

It's worth reminding ourselves of what all leaders are striving to achieve on the growth journey.

Building a long-term sustainable organisation is a primary goal. This is supported by the need to have a highly motivated, confident, flexible and performance-focused workforce. The working environment has to be right for them to deliver outstanding results. Innovation and the ability to adapt to and cope with change is a key requirement nowadays. Remaining pro-active in the face of changes in market conditions, economic events or legislation is also important. Recruiting and developing talent is essential. Retaining good people is a must have. Building trust and improving communication are critical to managing the day-to-day operational issues and 'growing pains' as they occur on the journey.

And you need to achieve all of this in a calm, professional and purposeful manner. Get it right and you have a better than even chance of success. The journey ahead is challenging and inspiring at the same time. All that is required is the will of your people and the use of the winning (formula)® performance framework.

The framework has six elements to it with a different leadership focus.

The winning (formula)® Framework

Framework		Leadership Focus
1	Research	• Reasons for signing up
	"The size of the opportunity"	• Challenges and issues • The landscape • The compelling vision
2	Strategy	• Critical success factors
	"The production of the route map"	• Culture and values • Link with operational performance • Blueprint for success
3	Engagement	• Engagement criteria
	"The buy-in and commitment to the growth plan"	• Workplace experience • The cultural architect • People survey
4	Motivation	• Performance criteria
	"The creation of the performance climate"	• Personal drive • Objectives and measures • Achievement, recognition, participation, growth
5	Development	• Structure of the organisation
	"The protection of systems, processes and people"	• Systems and processes • Skills and competencies • Lifelong learning
6	Ownership	• Trust in others
	"The maximisation of people potential"	• Pride in the journey and organisation • Confidence levels • Empowerment and autonomy

The Benefits of Using the Framework

Frameworks are widely used throughout the world to offer structure and support to individuals and organisations wishing to produce, construct or deliver a project. They are also used to help develop the knowledge, skills and behaviours required to achieve a desired level of personal performance.

The most effective frameworks offer a series of simple steps, concepts, approaches and insight which enables users to apply them effectively to achieve a required set of objectives.

The winning (formula)® is a performance development framework, designed for leaders to help them deliver growth for their organisation.

The personal benefit of using the framework is that it enables you as a leader to focus more effectively on the most important strategic and operational areas vital to securing sustainable growth for your organisation.

The framework also enables you to easily review your leadership performance, identify areas of development and implement improvements at a personal and operational level throughout your organisation.

It also enables you to shape your current and future strategies for the organisation around the framework. Linked to your unique challenges and ambitious plans for the future, the framework can be personalised to your organisation's exact needs, culture, values and people.

It is a powerful framework. Market conditions constantly change and the framework will enable you and your people to keep pace with the environment in which you operate. Your colleagues will remain focused and on track on your journey.

The framework also offers many benefits to your organisation. See opposite page.

Benefits to the Organisation

	Framework	Organisational Benefits
1	Research	• Development of the organisation vision
	"The size of the opportunity"	• Attraction and recruitment of talent • Involvement in the future plans • Clarity regarding direction and purpose
2	Strategy	• Agreement of culture and values
	"The production of the route map"	• Alignment of strategy to operational roles • Understanding of the plans for growth • Communication of personal contribution
3	Engagement	• Retention of internal talent
	"The buy-in and commitment to the growth plan"	• Improvement in leadership capability • Development of the communication grapevine • Identification of talent and future leaders
4	Motivation	• Improvement in overall morale
	"The creation of the performance climate"	• Development of performance management • Increase in management effectiveness • Workplace conducive to high performance
5	Development	• New ways of working identified
	"The protection of systems, processes and people"	• Improvement in operational efficiency • Sharing of knowledge and expertise • Performance skills and behaviors identified
6	Ownership	• Greater trust between leaders and others
	"The maximisation of people potential"	• Front-line autonomy and empowerment is achieved • Delivery of goals and objectives • Creation of an agile and sustainable organisation

It can form part of your day-to-day operation in two ways.

Option 1 – The Linear Approach

The framework can be used in a linear step-by-step way, starting with stage 1 (Research) and culminating in stage 6 (Ownership). It works best when there is an identified need to begin a new and exciting growth journey.

The linear approach is extremely effective on the back of a newly appointed leader heading up an organisation, or when a completely new strategic direction is identified as needed by the company. A new and more compelling vision is often required and if this is the case, the linear approach will produce immediate performance benefits.

The linear approach is also effective when an organisation feels it needs to review, refresh and re-energise itself in preparation for the future. Even though the organisation may be currently successful or has enjoyed a considerable amount of success in the past – a 'shot in the arm' is needed to reach the next level of growth.

A merger, acquisition, restructure or financial investment in the organisation offers other compelling reasons for using the linear approach. The enthusiasm generated by these events act as a real impetus to beginning a new and exciting journey. Momentum is used as a powerful force to drive the organisation forward.

The linear approach is particularly useful when momentum is required within the organisation to meet a series of commercial objectives over a short period of time. The winning (formula)® framework enables the organisation to get off to a great start and build on the accumulation of early successes by utilising the energy, commitment and power of the people – en masse – within the organisation.

Success breeds more success and obstacles, challenges and hurdles are easily overcome as a result of the power of momentum.

Growth and change are inextricably linked. You can not have one without the other. Using the framework in a linear fashion will also inspire your people to understand, support and perform in any change programme planned for your organisation.

Option 2 – The Tactical Approach

The framework can also be used by leaders tactically when there is an identified need to review and develop key aspects of the leadership and operational focus of the organisation on their existing growth journey.

Leaders may already have in place a strategy, a developed vision, a set of core values, performance objectives across the organisation, engagement initiatives and other important elements critical to delivering growth.

A tactical approach therefore may be more appropriate to their future needs. There is no point in unravelling the good work of the past, but it's important to constantly improve performance by refining and refocusing their people on key areas of importance throughout the organisation.

The winning (formula)® framework enables the leaders in the organisation to do this.

The six areas highlighted in the performance framework can therefore be developed as separate 'one-off' areas of focus.

The size of the opportunity may need to be further developed in line with any changes in the marketplace. The strategy may need to be 'fine-tuned' and relaunched to the workforce. Engagement levels may need to be assessed.

Motivation factors throughout the workforce constantly change. Learning is a big cultural challenge and will always require new ideas and input. Creating ownership across the organisation will always occupy the thoughts of leaders because of its importance.

The framework enables leaders to work on each area when they feel the need to on the journey.

Momentum still plays an important part in improving the performance of the organisation, particularly if you work fast and harness the energy of your people to focus on a specific element of the framework over a particular period of time.

Regardless of whether you choose a linear or tactical approach, the framework offers confidence, purpose and focus to you and your teams on the journey. In the hustle and bustle of leading an organisation it can often be difficult to 'see the woods for the trees'. The winning (formula)® framework enables you to do just that.

The framework also enables you to coach your people and your teams more effectively by focusing them on operational areas which have significant and lasting impact on the strategic direction of your organisation.

Overall the winning (formula)® framework enables everyone connected with the organisation to execute the strategy required to deliver growth.

Delivering Success
on the Journey

Fifty Important Points to Remember

Highlighted below are fifty important points for you to remember and focus on in your quest to build your own perfect pyramid.

1. Great journeys live long in the memory of those who participate in them.

2. Leadership is often defined by direction, influence and inspiration. Navigating the journey is the core skill requirement of the 21st century leader.

3. 'Navigation' requires a detailed understanding of the commercial landscape facing the organisation and the effective management of the human performance challenges on the journey.

4. Be honest with your people from the outset. Inform them of the challenges you may face, even if it means communicating bad or unpopular news. They won't thank you for any surprises later on in the journey.

5. Galvanising support from others is achieved by focusing on what is called the 'size of the opportunity' that exists for every individual who is connected with the organisation.

6. Linking the reasons why people should embark on the journey to the development of a compelling vision is arguably the most important task the leadership team in the organisation will ever carry out.

7. The vision document should highlight the destination, purpose,

workplace experience, challenges involved, support issued and the measure of success. It should be simple, ambitious, compelling and inspiring. This makes it easier to recruit and retain talented people on the journey.

8. Involving people in developing the vision document guarantees a high level of commitment at the start of the journey. Get the vision right and people will flock to join the organisation and sign up to the journey. Making it visually attractive to others is also useful. Pharaohs understood the importance and power of the verbal word, supported by the visual interpretation of the journey. The same principles apply to leaders in modern-day organisations.

9. Put your vision in writing and if reading it out aloud does not inspire you, it will never inspire others. This may seem an obvious thing to say, but the number of three-line visions we see that have the same effect as the outdated mission statement would surprise you. People don't understand them, they certainly don't believe in them and they often question the reasons for them.

10. Remember mission highlights purpose, vision highlights ambition and destination. A vision inspires, a mission rarely does.

11. Great journeys start off with purpose and very quickly develop a sense of belonging, which contributes towards the creation of an early critical mass of followers and advocates committed to the overall cause.

12. A great vision has a great purpose attached to it.

13. Identify the critical success factors required to realise your vision. Use them as the cornerstone of your day-to-day performance strategy. Your people must be able to relate each factor to their own job function. Watch how quickly they understand their role in your success when they do.

14. Reaching your destination will require a commitment to behaviours that are important to navigating the journey. Identify and agree the culture which best represents the needs of your organisation.

15. Your values should be used to underpin the culture and change in behaviour required on the journey.

16. Your success on the journey will be determined by the quality of leadership demonstrated throughout your organisation. To engage other people you will need the help of Cultural Architects. Identify, enlist and use them as early as possible.

17. Our clients call their 'Journey Map' a 'Blueprint for Success'. Issue a copy to everyone in the organisation. Use Cultural Architects in the communication and cascading process.

18. Your 'blueprint' offers a narrative about your future direction, which enables individuals to understand, trust and support your plans for growth.

19. The greater the number of Cultural Architects you have in the organisation, the stronger your leadership capability will be.

20. You should expect the same level of support to your future plans from external suppliers, partners and stakeholders as you would from your own colleagues. Issue everyone connected with your organisation a copy of your blueprint.

21. Carrying out employee surveys is critical to maintaining a high level of people engagement. If you believe morale and trust are low at the outset, always invite an external specialist to help you. Don't try to deliver the survey on your own. Your people won't give you the feedback you need to move forward.

22. Growth and change are inextricably linked. Resistance to change can be managed by using the contents included in your blueprint and the tactical use of the winning (formula)® framework.

23. Leaders should focus on inspiring and leading change first. Understanding, managing and coping with change will then follow.

24. Although it is natural for many people to resist change, new behaviour is often inspired by a sense of adventure.

25. Harness the power of vision and values to lead change, drive efficiency and deliver performance and success on the journey.

26. Success is achieved by maximising the talent and resources already in place in your organisation.

27. Developing an open, honest and positive communication grapevine is important to keeping your people on track.

28. You will at times need to recruit external talent to join you on the journey. The production and presentation of your blueprint will help you to do this.

29. Recruit and select individuals who are inspired by the vision and who wish to be part of your journey.

30. The journey won't be easy. If it were, then every organisation in the world would be hugely successful. It will involve hard work. Remind your people of this and of the benefits of being part of the unique growth journey.

31. Every single person brings something unique to the journey. Respect individuality whilst using the power of collective focus.

32. Acting fast, working hard and expecting the same from others is a useful operational mantra to have in the workplace.

33. Tough questions will be asked of your leadership team. (See the inside cover of this book). Be prepared to respond with the answers and build them into your strategy.

34. Great journeys involve an inspirational experience, challenges along the way and a desire to reach the destination with people you admire and respect.

35. Cascading five-year-plus growth plans is no longer appropriate and effective in today's fast moving, changing world.

36. Your journey timeline should be between three and five years maximum. A ten-year vision and plan – normally referred to as a long-haul trip – will require two or three separate short-haul journeys, with specific destination points, to enable your people to focus and deliver the performance you require.

37. Some of the leaders who deliver the vision will be different to the group who signed up at the beginning of the journey. Your operational personnel will also change.

38. Your landscape will constantly change and the use of the winning (formula)® performance framework will enable you to chart the correct course on the journey.

39. Each growth experience is unique, involving a different landscape and a different set of challenges on the journey.

40. Every challenge faced on the journey can be addressed by linking it to one of the six elements of the winning (formula)® framework.

41. Earning the right to grow starts with an operationally sound base, supported by a clearly understood strategy.

42. A measure of leadership effectiveness on the journey is the ability to achieve sustainable growth year after year.

43. Recognition as an agile and sustainable organisation is dependent on how responsive and empowered your people are at the front line.

44. If you can't do great things on the growth journey, do small things in a great way. Progress, momentum and success will be achieved.

45. The journey will involve setting and passing many milestones along the way. Celebrate every success, no matter how small it may be.

46. Everyone dreams of being part of something special – this applies to the world of work as much as it does to other aspects of life.

47. Creating a journey worth embarking on will make work and the workplace a more enjoyable experience.

48. Have fun. You might not like to admit it, but your people spend a large amount of their time at work. They deserve at least to enjoy it.

49. Great leaders create memorable journeys.

50. Issue all colleagues with a copy of *Building the Pyramid* to help describe the significance of your journey, their personal contribution and the rewards and satisfaction that are possible along the way.

Finally, there is no limit to what you can achieve. Imagine working in a high-performing organisation led by high-performing leaders, managed by high-performing managers supported by high-performing colleagues. The winning (formula)® will help you achieve this.

You instinctively know where you are going, but you need others to understand and commit to the destination too. You will occasionally need to stop and ask for directions along the way. That's not a bad thing.

The growth journey is unlike any other journey. You will be constantly be surprised by events as they unfold each and every day of your existence. But that's what great about it and one day you will look back and like the Pharaoh and his people you will say 'We built that!'

Sounds fantastic, doesn't it?

Best wishes on your journey wherever it may take you.

Leadership Checklist on the Journey

The following checklist has been produced as a useful reference guide for leaders tasked with using the winning (formula)® framework on their journey.

1. Research

Focus: the size of the opportunity on the journey

- Develop 'Imperatives for growth'
- Identify future challenges and human performance issues
- Understand the growth journey landscape
- Produce a compelling 'Vision' for the organisation
- Inspire individuals to sign-up on the journey

2. Strategy

Focus: the production of the route map

- Identify 'Critical success factors'
- Agree culture and values representative of the organisation's needs
- Demonstrate the link between 'Vision' and operational performance
- Produce a 'Blueprint for Success' document
- Inspire others to join you on the journey

3. Engagement

Focus: the buy-in and commitment to the growth plan

- Identify levels of support from others to the journey
- Increase people engagement levels
- Develop the organisation's communication grapevine
- Harness the role of the Cultural Architect
- Inspire others to support you on the journey

4. Motivation

Focus: the creation of a performance climate

- Identify barriers to motivation in the workplace
- Agree a 'high performance working' criteria for the organisation
- Build performance principles into the leadership operation
- Agree performance objectives for all personnel
- Inspire others to perform on the journey

5. Development

Focus: the protection of systems, processes and people

- Review operational efficiency throughout the organisation
- Innovate and seek ways of improving performance
- Agree skills and competencies for each job role
- Unlock the power of information and experience through 'learning'
- Inspire others to set new standards on the journey

6. Ownership

Focus: the maximisation of people potential

- Build trust with others in the organisation
- Develop a confident and empowered workforce
- Coach others to support an improvement in performance
- Create a high sense of pride in the organisation
- Inspire others to take personal responsibility on the journey

The Blueprint for Success

Delivering success on the journey by navigating the landscape will require a route map often referred to as a blueprint for success. The 'Blueprint for Success' is a simple, practical and easily understood document, designed for everyone connected with your organisation, which outlines your plans for the future and how you will go about achieving success and growth on the journey.

The 'blueprint' has many practical uses in the workplace.

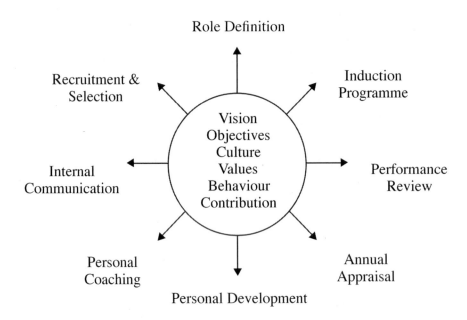

The blueprint should be produced using the development model shown opposite and the process highlighted in *Building the Pyramid*.

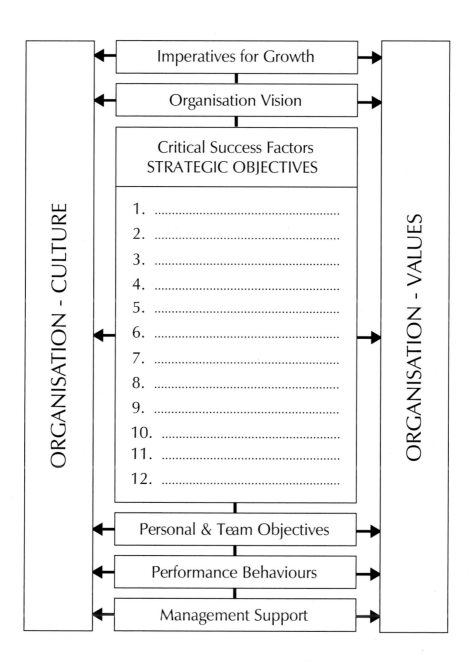

Modern-day Pharaohs and Their Journey

We have been privileged to work in collaboration with many modern-day Pharaohs in building their own unique pyramid. On each journey, the winning (formula)® has been instrumental in helping leaders and their teams navigate their course and reach their desired destination.

Fresenius Medical Care – creating a sustainable organisation

Fresenius Medical Care is a global leading provider of dialysis care. Peter O'Brien is the UK and Ireland Chief Executive.

A merger and the need to bring greater clarity regarding the future direction of the organisation were the primary reasons for embarking on a new journey. Other imperatives included the need to shape and lead a new culture with internal customer service, efficiency and quality identified as the main themes.

The journey focused on organisational development, change management and leadership development. Charting and navigating the company's new course involved understanding the challenges of growth and the development of a long-term vision. Cultural Architects were identified to lead and inspire others to develop new ways of working across the organisation.

At the beginning of the journey, Fresenius enjoyed a £40 million turnover. Fifteen years later its blueprint – including vision and culture – remains as relevant today. The company's clear sense of identity and belonging has delivered sustainability and growth success demonstrated through a market leading, £180 million plus turnover business delivered by 1100 employees. Peter describes the winning (formula)® as 'the organisational development equivalent of a multivitamin with the added benefits of a statin'.

Genesis Communications – delivering accelerated growth

Genesis Communications was one of the first companies in the UK to identify the enormous potential within the contract services sector of the mobile phone market. Ian Blackhurst was its pioneer and Managing Director.

The journey focused on the need for scaleability, the management of growing pains, a drive towards high performance working and operational efficiency, and the creation of a business that would attract the country's best talent.

The company's 'blueprint for success' had immediate impact. Genesis created a branch network of highly motivated sales professionals supported by a service and performance-focused head office operation. People engagement improved, retention levels of sales personnel increased and turnover accelerated from £7 million to £60 million in less than four years.

Navigating the journey and delivering the vision produced spectacular profit results, paving the way for the sale of the company for £31 million. Ian describes the winning (formula)® as 'a powerful approach which demonstrates how to deliver performance and efficiency throughout every area of the organisation'.

Alcontrol Laboratories – maximising talent on the journey

Alcontrol Laboratories is the market leading food, water and environmental testing organisation. Following an acquisition by Bridgepoint Capital, Managing Director Chris Boyes launched the company on what would be the start of a new and exciting journey for the organisation.

A need to build a self-sufficient, sustainable, market leading business was the main imperative for the company's initial journey. In order to secure funds required for the delivery of ambitious growth plans, it was also important to create value for shareholders.

The initial steps of the journey focused on maximising the service proposition of the company and the talent and expertise of its people to create a more competitive and successful organisation. Growth through acquisition formed a key element of Alcontrol's strategy and a new vision, strategic objectives and culture were developed to support future plans. Attracting and recruiting new talent contributed to a strengthening of the organisation across its UK sites.

The company began the journey with a year-on-year trading turnover of £17 million. Commitment to its blueprint and business excellence focus contributed towards a doubling of revenue and a five-fold return on investment for Bridgepoint. Alcontrol continues to enjoy market leading status. Chris described the winning (formula)® as 'an approach which maximises the use of the talent, knowledge, expertise and resources within the organisation'.

Phones 4U – aligning strategy to operational performance

Phones 4U is one of the longest standing and leading mobile phone retailers in the UK. Peter Green was the Managing Director of Corporate 4U and the man recruited by the board to improve the performance of the business.

Imperatives on the journey included the need to be profitable and self-funded within the Phones 4U group, and competitive and successful within the overall marketplace.

The journey focused on the alignment of a new strategic plan with the operational performance requirements of every individual in the organisation. A 'blueprint for success' – including a new vision for the Corporate 4U division, key areas of focus and values – was produced to communicate to 217 employees the new plans for growth. The 'blueprint' document explaining each individual's expected personal contribution became an integral part of the performance management process implemented by the leadership team.

Corporate 4U established itself in its marketplace and was sold by the Caudwell Group as part of a successful £1.5 billion disposal plan. Peter described the winning (formula)® as 'a simple and empowering approach to aligning strategy to operational performance'.

Gap Personnel – laying the foundations for future growth

Gap Personnel is one of the leading recruitment agencies in the UK. Gary Dewhurst is the founder and Chief Executive.

Staying ahead of its competitors and maximising the reputation and potential of the 'Gap brand' in the marketplace were the main reasons for embarking on the new journey. Enjoying 'preferred supplier status' with its clients and 'employer of choice' with others highlighted the ambition of the company.

The journey focused on utilising the energy, talent and resources within Gap to shape an exciting new direction for the organisation. The size of the commercial opportunity was identified by the leadership team, and a new vision for the company was produced.

Part of the new journey involved the development of a new performance culture, operational climate and unique customer service proposition. Encouraging its people to be 'independent, commercially focused, innovative and entrepreneurial' became central to its long-term growth strategy.

Gap Personnel began the journey with a trading turnover of £10 million per year. Laying the new foundations contributed to a 40% increase in revenue, 50% reduction in staff turnover and a 100% increase in customer retention in the first twelve months. The company's blueprint has lasted the test of time. Gap's vision of 'offering 100% unconditional commitment to excellence' has enabled the organisation to enjoy a turnover in excess of £90 million. Gary describes the winning (formula)® as 'an inspirational approach which motivates and inspires people to give their best'.

Chess – increasing people engagement levels

Chess operates in the telecom marketplace and is one of the UK's leading providers of business voice and data solutions. David Pollock is its founder and Chief Executive.

The ambition of the company is reflected in one of its imperatives for growth – 'we do not want to be known as the best of the best, we want to be known as the only ones who do what we do'.

Chess' journey – initially involving eighty employees – focused on creating a customer-focused and sustainable business driven by a 'buy and build' acquisition strategy. A blueprint for success – including a new vision – was produced with the leadership team. Achieving high levels of employee engagement was identified as important to the company's long term success. Cultural Architects played an active role in supporting the senior team with leadership and operational support, resulting in an open, vibrant and inspirational communication grapevine throughout the company.

Creating a climate of high-performance working has also been important to its success to date. The first leg of Chess' journey began with a trading performance of £9 million per year. Momentum played an important part in early growth. Turnover increased to £22 million in two years, customers increased by 112% and profits by 51%. The company continues to grow.

Chess is able to attract the best talent around because of its reputation as a 'great place to work'. The use of its 'blueprint' is self-evident throughout the business alongside the support for its core values – quality and spirit – which has contributed to the integration of over fifty acquisitions on the company's overall journey. Chess continues to enjoy market-leading status, employs over 250 people and enjoys an annual turnover exceeding £40 million. David describes the winning (formula)® as 'a process which brought structure to our thinking and greater focus to our organisation'.

Parasol – leading the change required to deliver success

Parasol is one of the leading employment services providers for the UK and international contracting industry. Rob Crossland is the founder and Chief Executive.

The journey began on the back of a management buy-out led by Rob and supported by private equity firm, Inflexion. Organisational development, business change and executive team changes formed part of the next leg of Parasol's new journey.

There was an identified need to harness the talent which existed within the business and inspire staff to perform and take Parasol to the next level of growth. Learning from the past, sharing best practice and continuing to solve old problems in new ways would be needed to develop an operational climate conducive to the needs of the company's growing band of customers.

Navigating the journey required a new vision, core values, culture and the identification of critical success factors. Parasol's blueprint for success inspired support from internal and external stakeholders.

Parasol's pioneering and progressive approach to 'doing the right thing' contributes to above average growth – 20% year-on-year – with an annual contracting turnover in excess of £350 million. Rob describes the winning (formula)® as 'a process which brings everyone together to formalise the way forward for the organisation'.

Sale Sharks Rugby Club – creating a climate of performance

Sale Sharks is one of the UK's leading rugby union clubs and has enjoyed a renaissance under the ownership of two entrepreneurial Pharaohs – Brian Kennedy and Ian Blackhurst. Both men faced the challenge of transferring their talent and commercial acumen to the sporting environment.

The journey focused on the development of a performance culture and the establishment of a leadership and commercial operation conducive to the needs of the ambitious new owners.

Their new vision and the production of their blueprint re-energised the club, attracted new talent and re-focused their leadership team and others on their expected performance contribution. Their work was rewarded with the first major trophy in the club's history, qualification for European competition followed by the Premiership trophy a few seasons later. Ian Blackhurst described the winning (formula)® as 'a performance approach applicable as much to the sporting as to the commercial world'.

Silverlining Furniture – harnessing the power of vision and values

Silverlining is the award-winning, luxury bespoke furniture brand found in palaces, embassies, museums, yachts and the private residences of the super rich. Mark Boddington is the entrepreneurial founder of the company.

The journey focused on clarifying Silverlining's future direction and the transformation of the company to meet the future needs of its exclusive and discerning clients. A new vision was developed – to become the most inspiring furniture brand of the 21st century – and a 'blueprint' was produced, highlighting the key areas of operational focus important to securing its success. The company's core values – excellence, passion and innovation – highlight the performance behaviours expected of everyone connected with the business.

Mark describes the use of the winning (formula)® as 'the most significant piece of work carried out by the organisation in its twenty-five year history'. Silverlining continues to blend design, craftsmanship, innovation and engineering to make its clients dreams come true.

My House Shared Services – delivering operational efficiency

My House Shared Services offer administration, information technology, compliance, purchasing, transport, finance, customer service and other support services to the £200 million portfolio of companies under the ownership and leadership of entrepreneur Ian Blackhurst. Organisations include market-leading brands such as Zenith Staybrite, Weatherseal, Penicuik and Job Worth Doing.

The journey involved the development of a shared services operation 'as a business in its own right' with a vision to support the group companies enabling them to focus on their own areas of expertise.

My House's future success would depend on a proposition matched by a service that was competitive and attractive to each group company. The business 'blueprint for success' communicated its offering to each organisation and highlighted the performance contribution expected from its head office personnel.

This innovative approach to delivering operational efficiency and servicing the needs of each company produced a saving of £1.2 million in the first year of its operation. The shared service operation has subsequently delivered significant cost benefits. Head of Shared Services, Tracey Talbot describes the winning (formula)® as 'an inspirational approach to focusing individuals on the behaviours required to deliver high performance working and efficiency in the workplace'.

Feedback from others

We are privileged to have received positive feedback from other recognised bodies and leading authorities on our clients' journeys.

Investors in People (IIP) is an acknowledged standard and accreditation process popular with thousands of organisations in the UK. The winning (formula)® framework has enabled many organisations to achieve IIP status. Judging Assessor John Wilson described the 'blueprint for success' as 'a quite extraordinary document, in its comprehensive content, the fact that staff were involved in its compilation and the way everyone has bought into it as an operational bible'. He also commented "clearly it is not paying lip-service to corporate ideals – everyone understands how they contribute to the success of the company".

The winning (formula)® has also twice won a prestigious UK National Training Award for 'design originality, delivery and the performance results achieved with our clients'. Their judging panel described the framework as 'demonstrating the power of learning in a business environment leading to overarching business benefits'. As you can imagine we are proud of this recognition.

We also like the comment received from Charles Handy who on reading the lessons from the journey described them as 'common sense' and added 'but as we both know commonsense is not very common'.

Common sense has always played a huge part in the design of the framework and the powerful use it brings to each organisation.

Acknowledgements

The writing and completion of *Building the Pyramid* has involved a journey similar to that of Smendes and his people in the kingdom.

The desire to produce a unique piece of work was the driving force behind the interpretation and communication of the winning (formula)® performance framework. Many of the lessons highlighted in the book have applied throughout the creative and production process including the importance of vision, strategy, engagement, performance, learning, teamwork and collaboration.

My grateful thanks go to Nicola Bramhall, Adele Ventre-Downey, Lloyd East and Carl Fitzsimons for their professional and personal input towards the completion of the book. I have found their guidance and advice invaluable.

I would like to pay tribute to the professionalism of the winning (formula)® team involved in the production of the publication.

My thanks go to Jo Russell for her support and contribution towards the editing of the original storyline and other sections of this publication. I also wish to thank Chay Hawes for his creative interpretation of the Pharaoh's journey and the design of the cover of the publication.

Thanks also to Sylvia Worth. Building the Pyramid is supported by a wide range of leadership development and growth products. She deserves a special mention for her editorial support towards our growing portfolio. I am also grateful for her support in completing the publication.

The winning (formula)® entered the business marketplace in 1995. Since then, over 1,000 organisations and 100,000 professionals have supported the framework and applied the lessons highlighted in this book. My thanks go to each and every client for allowing us to share our approach with them in their organisations. I am also indebted to their critical feedback over the years regarding the relevance, delivery and outcomes achieved as a result of its use.

In particular, I would like to say a special thanks to long-standing client and entrepreneur Ian Blackhurst who has supported the winning (formula)® by using it in all of his companies since the late nineties. He regularly champions our approach and I am greatly appreciative of this.

Frank Price, author of *Right First Time* and *Right Every Time* has been a major influence throughout the winning (formula)® journey. Sadly Frank is no longer with us. Before he passed away, his insight and encouragement was a source of great inspiration. I miss him very much.

I am also grateful to author and philosopher Charles Handy – my professional hero and a major influence in my career – who was kind enough to read my pre-publication draft of *Building the Pyramid*. I would like to thank him for the encouragement, guidance and advice given to me regarding the content and structure of the final version of the book. His input and support means a great deal to me.

Finally, my thanks and love go to the most important person in my life, my wife Linda. She has been with me since the birth of the winning (formula)® and has experienced close hand the highs and lows of the journey. Without her constant encouragement *Building the Pyramid* would not have been possible.

the winning *(formula)*®

The winning (formula)® performance framework described in *Building the Pyramid* is available to you and your organisation in the following flexible delivery formats:

- Executive Coaching Programmes
- Leadership & Management Workshops
- Team Building Events
- Licensed Publications & Resources
- Train the Trainer
- Conference and Keynote Speaking

www.the-winning-formula.com

About the Author

John Stein is the founder of the winning (formula)® and a champion of growth.

He is widely recognised as a leading authority on the human performance issues facing organisations on the growth journey, and has dedicated his career to working with leaders and their teams to build agile, successful and sustainable organisations.

In a world of constantly changing commercial landscapes, he focuses on developing the navigation skills of the 21st century leader. He is often described as an 'organisational lighthouse keeper' by his clients and peer group as a result of the knowledge, support and guidance he is able to offer them on their unique journey.

He has worked with small, medium-size and large organisations and has the rare privilege of experiencing the highs and lows of the growth journey with ambitious founders, entrepreneurs, chief executives, directors and their teams.

John is an award-winning practitioner, conference speaker and facilitator of leadership away-days and strategy events. He is able to engage with individuals at all levels in any organisation, and uses a unique blend of research data, humour, pragmatism and commonsense to inspire others to maximise their potential.

For more information about John and the winning (formula)®

Website: www.the-winning-formula.com
Twitter: JohnStein_TWF
Linkedin: linkedin.com/in/johnsteintwf

John can be contacted by email at john@the-winning-formula.com